ZION
Champion for
GOD

To order additional copies of *Zion—Champion for God*, by Joy Matthews, call 1-800-765-6955.

Visit us at www.reviewandherald.com for information on other Review and Herald® products.

ZION
Champion for
GOD

Joy J. Matthews
With Helen Heavirland

REVIEW AND HERALD® PUBLISHING ASSOCIATION
HAGERSTOWN, MD 21740

The author assumes full responsibility for the accuracy of all facts and quotations as cited in this book.

The places, people, and events of this story are true. Most names, some details, and a few places have been changed to protect anonymity.

This book was
Edited by Jocelyn Fay
Designed by Pierce Creative/Matt Pierce
Cover photos by Jerry Vavra Photography/Zion and Joy Matthews
and Joel Springer/blue ribbon
Typeset: Bembo 11/14

PRINTED IN U.S.A.
08 07 06 05 04 5 4 3 2 1

R&H Cataloging Service
Matthews, Joy and Helen Heavirland
Zion—champion for God.

1. Schnauzers. I. Heavirland, Helen. II. Title.

636.73

ISBN 0-8280-1816-2

Dedication

To teenagers everywhere
(my favorite people)—
and to all who are teenagers at heart!

Contents

Why Am I on This Planet?

WHY AM I EVEN ON THIS PLANET, GOD?" I whispered the words in desperation.

The blue sky didn't cave in. Lightning didn't strike the big old maple I leaned against. But the front door banged.

"There goes the pretty one." I sighed. "Out with her latest date."

My twin sister was beautiful. She always had a sparkle in her eye. She was fun, boisterous, witty. People loved hanging around her.

Then there was me. A plain Jane. Mousy brown hair. Dull blue eyes. No fun. No talents. No special abilities. So bashful no one even knew *if* I was around . . . except Toby. I threw my arms around my brother's dog and buried my face in his warm neck.

"Why is there no fun for me? Will I ever find a purpose for *my* life? Will I ever be happy?"

Toby's tail thumped against my leg.

I leaned forward and looked him in the eye. "I can't even have a dog of my own," I grumbled. "Why can my brother have a dog, but I can't?"

Just thinking about it, I clenched my teeth so tight my jaws hurt. "I'm 16," I muttered, "and my best friend is a dog. A dog that doesn't even belong to me."

I hugged the big black and brown mutt again. "Not putting

you down, Toby. You and God are pretty good listeners. But God doesn't seem to answer. And you're gone with my brother as much as you're here. I want a dog that's all my own." Toby lifted his head and rolled big brown eyes up toward me. I went on: "And I want a horse, too."

I leaned back against the rough maple trunk, my arm across Toby's shoulder. My eyes gazed, unseeing, toward the sky. I dreamed of the horse I'd have . . . someday.

I thought back to a school outing that spring. It was supposed to be an every-horse-plods-in-a-line kind of ride. But at least I got to ride. I wore hand-me-down cowboy boots.

Lance, the stable owner, scrutinized each of us head to toe before he assigned a horse. He glanced at me and headed to the corral. Halfway there he turned. He squinted toward me, then hurried on and chose a bright-eyed chestnut mare.

Moments later he tied her reins to a post by me. He patted the mare's flank. "Lightning'll give ya a good ride."

When I rubbed Lightning's muzzle, she looked directly at me. I patted her shoulder and spoke softly. "I'm delighted to get to ride you, Lightning!" She twitched an ear. I chattered on as I stroked and patted her. "I love the sight of manes flying, the *da-dum, da-dum, da-dum* of galloping hooves, the sense of oneness between a horse and rider. But now, I won't just see it on a silver screen."

When a horse was tied to the post by each student, Lance showed us how to get into the saddle. I slipped my left foot into the stirrup, grabbed the saddle horn, and swung my right leg over Lightning's back. I'd seen it on TV so often that it almost felt natural. A thrill surged through me as I sat atop the powerful beast.

One by one, Lance untied the horses and handed the reins to their riders. As he handed the reins to me he said, "You bring up the rear. OK?"

"Sure."

After a brief riding lesson, we plodded in line down a narrow wooded trail. Lightning edged closer to the horse ahead, but always slowed when I tightened the reins.

When we broke out of the woods and started across an open meadow, Lightning took off at a gallop. She passed two other horses like she thought she were racing . . . and winning. I recovered from the surprise and pulled the reins. Lightning didn't let up. I sensed she'd like to feel me slide off right over her rump. I poked my toes deeper into the stirrups, tightened my knees to her sides, and kept a steady pull on the reins. We flew past another horse. Another wooded section lay ahead. It looked like the trail was narrower than before. My heart pounded faster than Lightning's hooves. *What should I do?*

Suddenly I recalled an idea from somewhere in the process of reading everything I could get my hands on about horses. I pulled the left rein. Lightning veered left off the path, into the meadow. I kept up a steady pull. We flew in a wide circle. I pulled harder. The circle shrank and she slowed a smidgen. I tugged even harder. The circle tightened. I pulled harder and Lightning slowed into a tighter and tighter circle until she walked in a ring hardly any further across than her length. I tugged at both reins . . . and she stopped.

The gallop had been a shock—and a thrill. I took a deep breath, then patted Lightning's shoulder. "You know, Lightning, I'm still delighted to get to ride you!" I clucked my tongue and loosened the reins. "Let's go girl. We'd better catch up with the others."

Lightning galloped again, but she responded to the slightest tension on the reins. We raced toward the trail and headed in the direction the others had gone. I delighted in the fresh outdoor fragrance and the sweaty horse smell. In the *clap, clap, clap* of Lightning's hooves on the trail. In the jouncing on her back.

When we came into the next clearing, one of my classmates was off her horse, but trying to get on. The last of the other horses was just entering another wooded area ahead. I tightened Lightning's reins, and she slowed obediently.

Somehow, the girl trying to get on her horse dropped the reins. Her horse raced off through the meadow. The girl screamed and took off running after the rest of the group.

Lightning and I galloped after the loose horse. As we neared, the other horse slowed to a trot. I reined Lightning in till her pace was barely faster than the other horse's. I spoke softly as we approached. After several minutes alongside the other horse, I leaned over and grabbed its reins.

And this was supposed to be a boring, plod-plod-plod, follow-the-leader kind of ride, I thought as we trotted after the others. *But it's been exciting!*

Before long I saw the others in the distance. They were stopped. The girl who'd lost her horse was talking to Lance.

"Here he comes," another classmate hollered. They all looked up. Lance's mouth dropped open when he caught sight of us.

"Thank you, Ma'am!" Lance smiled when I handed him the reins. "You sure saved me a bundle of trouble! Why, when Possum gets loose he wanders all over tarnation. It could have taken me hours to find him! How'd you catch him, anyway?"

I told him.

"Good job," he said. "'Possum's usually kind of skittish when he gets out in the open. Did he give you any trouble?"

"No."

"You're good with horses if you could catch Possum like that. You've ridden a lot, haven't you?"

I snickered. "Only in my dreams."

Lance's eyes lost their sparkle. His smile disappeared. "How much *have* you ridden?"

"Two brief rides where everyone just plodded along in a row."

"That's all?"

"Yeah."

"You're not jivin' me?"

"No."

Lance rolled his eyes upward. He looked back at me and shook his head. "I took one look at you and thought, *There's experience.* I'd never have given you Lightning if I'd known you were a beginner. She's barely broke. Her name ain't Lightning for nothin'!" He sighed again. Did *she* give you any trouble?"

"Well, she took off on a gallop and wouldn't stop."

"Wha'd ya do?"

I told him about the shrinking circles.

Lance shook his head. "You're a natural." His eyebrows raised. "May as well let you stay on Lightning at this point. You called her bluff and you won. She respects you now."

I sat tall in the saddle. It was a wonderful day.

Toby barked toward the street, jerking my mind back to the present. A neighbor boy waved as he rode by on his bike.

Spoiling Toby. The neighbor's dog looks on.

I thought about Lance's comment—"You're a natural." Thought of the tricks I'd taught my brother's dog. Not everyone could sense an animal's heart like I seemed to be able to. Might I have a talent with animals?

I pondered that a moment. *Weird,* I thought. *Even if I do have a talent with animals, what good would that do anyone?*

A few puffy white clouds drifted behind the leaves of the maple tree, then out again. "God, I understand I can't have a horse in my bedroom in Minneapolis. It'll be forever till I get a horse. But could I have a dog?"

What breed would I choose if I could have any dog I wanted? I wondered. *German shepherd? Collie? Chow? Elkhound? Doberman? Definitely a* big *dog.*

A few weeks later a Brittany spaniel showed up at the neighbor's. I petted him. His ribs didn't have much cover. His brown eyes looked up longingly. He leaned into my leg as if to savor every iota of attention and tease me into a few more pats.

The neighbors looked for his owners.

I started calling the dog Freckles. Every day he and I got a little better acquainted. He would come when I called and sit on command. He was a quick learner. I taught him to shake hands. Whenever I went out our door, he bounded toward me as if I were a long lost friend.

"Well, Joy," the neighbor said one evening, patting Freckles on the head, "we've tried everything and can't find this dog's owner. He sure likes you. Would you like to have him?"

"Yes!" My heart raced. Then a lump formed in my throat. "But I'll have to check with my folks."

I took Freckles home. "Have you noticed this dog over at the neighbor's?" I asked hesitantly.

"Yeah," Dad answered. "Nice-looking dog."

"He's a really sweet dog," I hurried on. "Gentle, obedient, smart . . ."

"Uh-h-h-h . . ." An I-just-caught-on look crossed Dad's face. He put up his hand as if to stop traffic. "Hold everything." The tone of his voice hardened. "You can't keep him, Joy."

I guess he hadn't forgotten the other dogs that had wandered in and I'd tried to adopt. "But he's different," I said. "He's obviously been taken care of. He's well behaved."

"No."

I didn't usually beg. I liked to please people, not to bug them. "But I felt desperate. But I need a dog. And he needs a home. He could sleep by my bed. I'll figure out a way to earn the money for his food. I can—"

"No."

"But—"

"The answer is *no!*"

The lump in my throat felt like a watermelon. My chest felt like something inside was dying. I swallowed hard. When I finally spoke, my voice was soft but strangely firm. "When I get married, I'm going to choose a man who likes animals as much as I do!"

Weird Talent

FOR THREE HOURS AFTER SCHOOL every day, I pasted backs on one book after another at a bindery. The paycheck helped with necessities. The summer after high school graduation I was a server in a restaurant. I was proud of the job I did and the compliments I received. But my favorite time of day was training Toby to roll over or fetch. Or taking him for a run. Or leaning against the old maple trunk reading a book about horses or dogs with Toby nudging my hand every so often to keep me petting him.

When I left for college, I missed Toby terribly. When I started dating Del, he had a Chihuahua. Before long the little dog snuggled in my lap every chance he got. When Del and I married, it was fun having Scamp prance around our apartment, but he was a far sight from "big." And I still longed to have a horse and a dog that was *mine.* It would be fine if they were friendly and civilized to other people. But I wanted an animal whose *first* allegiance was to me.

Eventually I got *my* first dog—I rescued a miniature schnauzer, Rebel, who'd been chained outside for a year and a half. My heart went out to him. From the first, every morning I held Rebel, gently stroked him, and told him softly what a fine dog he was and what a nice dog he would be. Before many weeks passed, he bounced around my ankles or jumped onto my lap.

Besides being my special pet, initially Rebel provided quite a bit of humor around our house. Some of his antics resulted from his lack of exposure to the world most puppies explore. Bred to be guard dogs, schnauzers rarely cower from anything. Rebel attacked the flyswatter, the broom, the vacuum cleaner . . . until he learned they'd not be used against him nor anyone else in the family he'd adopted.

On one of our first excursions after Rebel arrived, we went to a secluded area by a lake. He sniffed the picnic site, then spotted several gulls floating 70 feet from shore. Taking his watchdog role seriously, he ran toward the creatures that sat on the shiny "ground." A moment later, he disappeared, then surfaced, sputtering and sneezing.

The gulls bobbed on the water, undisturbed. Still dripping, Rebel eyed them like an agent casing a suspect. When he could stand it no longer, he raced after them again. Again he came up sputtering and sneezing.

Rebel kept an eye on those creatures that relaxed on shiny blue surfaces, but he never tried chasing them again.

I enjoyed Rebel, but he didn't have any manners. One evening I noticed an ad in the newspaper for a Dog Obedience Class. I showed it to Del. "Do you think Rebel is too old and independent to learn from a class?" I asked.

"He's learned a lot since he came to live with us," Del said.

"Yes, he has," I agreed. "It's worth a try."

At the class, 50 miles from home, Rebel held back from the other dogs, especially the St. Bernard puppy that bounced around like a loose cannon. But I spoke softly to Rebel. He calmed down somewhat, and we did our best to follow the trainer's instructions.

We practiced with a leash several times every day. By the next Monday Rebel traipsed along beside me on his leash like he'd been doing it all his life.

Whatever the lesson, we practiced hard each week. I hadn't had as much fun since my high school day on horseback. On the final night, after all 26 dogs and their masters had been tested, Rebel and I got the high-point trophy.

I was excited—and shocked. I had a hard time believing I could do anything well.

Rebel and I attended an advanced class. We continued working hard. The more time Rebel and I spent together, the more he trusted me. As trust grew, the more quickly he learned and the more fun the learning was for both of us. We walked away with the trophy again.

One evening when I was outside with Rebel, I sensed a question in my mind as clearly as if someone had spoken. *When did you start loving Rebel?*

"When I saw him," I answered.

Was he well-behaved?

"Certainly not!" I responded. "He was a pain at first."

Did he have to earn your love?

"No."

God is your Master. Do you think He is less loving than you are?

I'd sung "Jesus Loves Me" from cradle roll. But I'd never felt good enough to deserve His love. As I thought about God as my Master and about my love for Rebel, I began to believe that maybe God really could love me. And I began talking with Him more. And listening.

Around home, Rebel was a pleasure. We bought a female miniature schnauzer, Tory, and began raising pups. I took Tory, then some of her pups, through obedience classes. We adopted a couple Great Dane pups, and I took them to obedience class also.

After moving to the country, I prayed every now and then, "God, I love my family. I enjoy our menagerie of dogs, and I don't want to seem ungrateful . . . but I'd still really like to have a horse."

In time we bought 8-year-old Prince. *If I can conquer this pony,* I thought, *then I'll be ready to tackle a full-size horse.* I was a total greenhorn at horse training. I depended on love, on the same principles that worked for training dogs—kindness and consistency. Prince and I learned together. A big black and white Appaloosa came next.

One day at the rodeo grounds where we kept our horses, I heard a *thud . . . thud.* I looked around. Above the wall of a stall, a two-by-four swung down out of sight. I heard the thud again. I walked closer. A man swung the board till it thudded again across the neck of a beautiful, very pregnant bay mare with flowing black mane and tail. The man swung the two-by-four again. The mare flinched as the board landed between her ears.

My heart raced. I looked around for someone to come to the horse's rescue. No one else was on the rodeo grounds. The board raised. It hit the mare on the head again. A fire flamed up in my chest. I had to do something. I ran to the fence. "What are you doing?" I demanded.

"Trying to break her," the man with the two-by-four snapped.

My heart thumped in my throat.

"I've got to sell her," the man went on, "but she won't do nothin'." He dropped the board, stomped off, and roared away in his pickup truck.

That evening Del and I figured our finances down to the last penny. The next morning I was back at the rodeo grounds. The ornery man was with the bay mare when I arrived. My palms sweat till I could barely hold the wad of cash. I swallowed the lump in my throat and strode over to the pen. "What would you take for this horse right now?"

"She ain't broke, lady. Won't do ya no good like this."

"How much?"

We settled on a price. I took Shannon's reins and patted her shoulder. "Let's go, girl," I said. She followed me to our corral.

Shannon was a Welsh-Pony of the Americas cross. Thirteen hands tall—about halfway between the size of our pony and our Appaloosa. As I patted her muzzle, she leaned her head toward me. "No one will ever hurt you again as long as I'm around," I whispered into her velvet ear.

Within days Shannon recognized the sound of our car. She'd look up and come running as I drove up. As soon as I was out of the car, she'd nicker and watch me approach. She'd meet me at the gate and nuzzle my neck.

Riding Shannon.

Three weeks after we purchased Shannon, her former owner saw me riding her. His mouth dropped open. He came closer and watched for a few minutes. "How'd ya get her to this point already?" he asked.

I looked him squarely in the eye. An edge of contempt oozed out of my voice. "A little love and kindness, sir."

Del and I rode together every chance we got. Often as we headed out into the country, we rode through a small community of migrant workers. Children would scamper away chattering. They'd be back in an instant with other children in tow. "Look!" they'd shout, pointing. We'd smile and wave, and they would, too.

One afternoon I rode alone through the migrant community. As the children gathered, memory took me back to my own childhood. I'd loved horses since I first saw one. I'd longed to ride one, to sit on one, to even touch one. *There could be a child here,* I thought, *who wants to touch a horse as much as I did.* I stopped, climbed off Shannon, and held the reins. "Want to pet the horse?" I asked.

"Yes!" A choir of voices responded. "Yes! Oh, can we?"

"Sure," I said, motioning them to come.

Children patted or stroked Shannon's muzzle and side, chattering with excitement. *Kids and animals just seem to go together,* I thought.

One day when I telephoned the dog obedience trainer to register a puppy for a class, she didn't just happily sign us up as she always had. "Joy," she said, "why don't you teach the class yourself, there in your town?"

"Oh, I couldn't do that."

"Sure, you could," she insisted. "You've been through my classes over and over. You've seen everything I do."

"B-b-but . . ." Just the thought of my teaching a class made my voice quaver.

"Besides," the trainer continued, "it didn't matter what dog you brought. Every time you came, you took the high-point trophy. It wasn't because every dog you brought was smart. Some were pretty impossible cases. You simply have a knack with dogs."

Caesar, a Great Dane, was allowed to place his paws on my shoulder only when I invited him to. He was one of the menagerie of dogs with which I earned the high-point trophy.

The next afternoon, atop Shannon, I prayed, "God, could I teach a dog-training class? Is that something You'd want me to do?"

As I pondered, Shannon's *clop, clop, clop* eased my mind. I basked in the sun's warmth on my back. I took a long, deep breath and closed my eyes to savor the hint of prairie's spring growth.

A jumble of children's screeches jolted me. From the midst of the clamor I heard, "Look! Horse!" Children ran from every direction to the edge of the road. "Look! Look! Horse!"

Of course we stopped. The children's eyes danced. They patted Shannon and chattered with glee.

After that, whenever I rode through the migrant community, children came running and I almost always let them pet my gentle Shannon. Each time the thought *Kids and animals just seem to go together,* grooved itself more deeply into my thinking.

A few weeks later my hands shook as I stood before five men and women with their canine companions. When I opened my mouth, my voice trembled.

The second session was easier. Week after week I saw the progress the dogs and their owners made. Teaching energized me. Slowly, the initial nervousness subsided.

"I just can't thank you enough, Joy," a lady said one evening. Her Dalmatian stood contentedly by her side. "I was so frustrated I was about ready to give my dog to the first person who'd take her. Now we're having fun together. She's wonderful! Thank you so-o-o much!"

I could see the difference. And not just for this pair. By and large the dogs wanted to please their masters. And their masters were enjoying their dogs.

I am making their lives better by sharing what I've learned, I realized. *Thank You, God.*

On the last night of class, I received lots of thank yous and several owners signed up for an advanced class. A sense of accomplishment welled up inside me. And I heard God whisper, *Joy, you're good at this.*

"God," I prayed, "understanding animals always seemed like a weird talent. Can You use it somehow?"

So Much for That Dream

ONE DOG TRAINING CLASS led to another . . . and another.

I kept plenty busy. Besides teaching classes, I learned to groom different breeds of dogs. Soon I had as many clients as I could handle. I also learned to evaluate puppies to determine what kind of temperament they'd have. Eventually I began training dogs one at a time in their homes. It felt good to help dogs and their owners.

I also continued raising puppies and training them. I showed Rebel in dog fun shows and got to know other people who loved dogs. I did a lot of observing, asked a load of questions, and learned a bundle. At the fun shows I often noticed children longing to pet the dogs. One day a thought came out of nowhere—*Since kids and animals just seem to go together, maybe I could help teach Vacation Bible School . . . with a dog.*

Where'd that thought come from? I wondered.

Even after Rebel died, the idea kept cropping up in my mind. "God," I prayed, "is this from You?"

One day I mentioned the idea to a friend. A few months later she telephoned and asked, "Remember the idea of bringing a dog to Vacation Bible School?"

"Yes."

"Well, I just took on Vacation Bible School. And you're on!"

"But I'm not ready."

"You've got a month. You can get ready."

"But right now I don't have a dog that would work for that."

"You train dogs. Someone must have a dog you could bring."

I thought about Casey, a sweet 5-month-old Golden Retriever I'd been training. She obeyed several commands. She loved to please me. Her owners agreed to let her visit Vacation Bible School.

When Casey and I walked into the church on Monday, the children gasped. Their eyes lit up. *This was a great idea!* I thought.

Casey sat very still beside me as I talked to the children. She obeyed "Casey, stay" when I walked across the platform. "Casey, come," I said. She came. "Casey, sit." She sat.

At the end, I told the children they could come pet Casey gently. The teachers brought the children a few at a time.

I knelt by Casey. As the children stroked her, she leaned against me, looking up at me with pleading eyes.

On Tuesday Casey held back on her leash when we got to the church door. When we went through, the children's eyes lit up. "Casey!" they called. "Casey!"

Again Casey sat beside me as I talked to the children. But when I walked across the platform, then said, "Casey, come," she looked at me. She looked at the children. She looked back at me. Finally, trembling, she walked to me.

"Casey's not used to a crowd," I explained to the children. "She's frightened. I wanted her to do some other things for you, and I wanted to let you all pet her again, but she's too nervous. Maybe she'll feel less afraid tomorrow."

But Wednesday was worse. Casey froze. She wouldn't obey at all. She just stood beside me and trembled.

I couldn't do that to a dog. I didn't bring Casey back.

Riding Shannon that afternoon, I prayed, "God, it didn't

work with Casey and the kids. Was Vacation Bible School my idea, not Yours? Should I forget it?"

But the children's excitement when they saw the dog, the delight when they got to pet Casey, wouldn't leave my mind.

Friday evening, the children brought family and friends to a final program. As pictures of the week's activities showed on a screen, children pointed and whispered loudly to the grown-ups beside them, "I did that," or "Look, that's me!" When a shot of Casey showed, children from around the sanctuary spontaneously chanted, "Ca-sey! Ca-sey! Ca-sey!"

"God," I prayed, "the kids loved it. The dog hated it. Should I pursue it?"

I sensed God whisper *Yes.*

It was clear I'd have to have my own dog if I were going to take a dog to Vacation Bible School again. What would the dog need to be like? *A dog that's gentle. A dog that likes people. One that learns quickly. One that will love and obey me. One that is beautiful. And it* has *to like people!*

I still liked big dogs best. And a big dog would be easier for the children to see. I studied the breeds that interested me.

Giant schnauzer, I finally decided. I sensed peace about the decision. A male, I decided. They're generally bigger, more impressive.

When I shared my dream with Del, he was all for it. Sometimes the memory of Casey trembling beside me would tempt me to forget teaching children with a dog. Then I'd remember the children's delight.

Somewhere along the line when I talked to God about taking a dog to Vacation Bible School, the assumption changed from *if* I do it to *when* I do it. One morning during my prayer time, a thought surprised me: *Zion. His name will be Zion.*

A majestic name, I thought. *A name that denotes power. That reminds me of heaven. A name that reminds me God is the center of this, not me.*

"But 'Zion' for a dog?" I asked God. "Would that be sacrilegious?"

I studied and prayed and asked my husband, my pastor, and some of my friends. I sensed that the name was right and decided that indeed, Zion would be the name—*when* God arranged for the dog.

The months slipped by. I talked to God about the dog He was going to provide. I trained and groomed dogs and saved as much as I could toward the purchase price of a giant schnauzer. I checked with Charles and Lorraine, whom I'd met when I had Rebel. Friendly and helpful, they were breeders who had a healthy line of giant schnauzers with gentle temperament.

"We don't have any puppies and we're not expecting any," Lorraine said. "But Kathy bought one of our females. Her dog will be having puppies in a few weeks."

My mind raced. I'd seen the mother at dog shows. And I knew Kathy, too.

Lorraine went on, "The father is our Schmidt."

I'd seen Schmidt. He was a big, happy-go-lucky giant schnauzer with a heart of gold. That meant the puppies' parents and grandparents all had good temperament. Unfortunately, Schmidt was homely as a mud fence.

I gave Kathy a call.

"Yes, we are expecting puppies in about five weeks," she said.

We talked about the mother and the expected puppies. I told Kathy about my Vacation Bible School plans. "Joy," she said, "you can have the pick of the litter."

That clinched the deal for me. To get to choose my puppy first was wonderful! When I offered to evaluate and temperament-test the litter of puppies, she was grateful.

Kathy finally called. Nine puppies. Seven males.

My heart beat faster. With seven male puppies to choose from, surely there'd be the perfect pup to fulfill my mission.

In August, when the pups were 8 weeks old, I went to test them and choose my Zion.

There they were—nine balls of soft black fur, nine square muzzles with beards already showing, nine shiny black noses, 18 bright black eyes. At 8 weeks, they were each about the size of a full-grown miniature schnauzer.

To evaluate the puppies, I watched how they related to each other and how they responded to me, a stranger. I checked how they reacted to a moving object and to surprise. I held the puppies on their backs and watched how agitated they got. I spent hours checking out the nine pups.

Several of the male puppies were alert, intelligent. But one was a standout—beautiful, perfect build, perfect gait. *That's the one!* I thought.

A question about his temperament pawed at my thinking.

B-b-but . . . it'll be . . . OK, I told myself. *He's so-o-o beautiful!*

Finally I was ready to give Kathy my report. But I was most excited to tell her which puppy I chose. I picked up the attractive pup. "This is the one I want," I told her.

"You can't have him," she responded. "I'm going to keep that one."

What Do You Really Want?

"YOU CAN'T HAVE HIM. I'm going to keep that one." The breeder's words caught me totally off guard. My jaw must have dropped a foot. My thoughts whirled. *She said I could have the pick of the litter. She didn't say she was even interested in keeping one. But . . . they are her puppies.*

"O-OK," I choked out.

"The father's owners are coming after their puppy in the morning," Kathy said. "You can choose yours after that."

In my camper I was still reeling from the shock. "God," I prayed, "what's going on?"

What do you really want? I heard Him whisper.

"Good temperament," I replied. "A dog that will be good with kids."

I thought back over the hours observing the pups. Most had a decent disposition. But I had to consider looks, too. I needed a dog that would attract the kids. The one I'd chosen would be a great show dog, too.

"Man looketh on the outward appearance . . .

". . . but the Lord looketh on the heart." I finished the sentence from 1 Samuel 16:7 without even thinking. The blood drained from my face. I wanted a puppy to work for God. But when it came right down to choosing which puppy, I had depended on my own wisdom. I hadn't even asked for God's wisdom. I considered temperament. But when it came to the final decision, I chose on the basis of looks.

"God, forgive me," I prayed. "Which puppy is right for the job You want done?"

I couldn't have the best-looking puppy. One other was good-looking, but he was apt to be extremely active. He'd probably have trouble settling down, especially when he was with a group of children. But he was such a handsome little fellow. No doubt he could win a championship.

Another puppy was a standout in temperament. Easygoing but alert. Gentle but confident. Laid-back but intelligent. Unfortunately, he looked like his dad—downright homely.

What a choice! One was good looking but probably would be a pain to live with. One had a heart of gold but was homely.

What do you really want? I heard God whisper again.

If the third puppy had been even mediocre in looks, the decision wouldn't have been so tough. But if I chose the homely one, I might as well forget dog shows.

"Seek ye first the kingdom of God" [Matthew 6:33, KJV].

The homely puppy would be fun. There was a mellow sweetness about him, yet he was alert and playful. Surely he'd be good with children. Besides, dog shows took a lot of time and energy.

"I'm going to choose the 'ugly duckling' puppy," I said aloud. A smile came to my face . . . and to my heart. Somehow the choice just felt right.

Then another thought exploded in my mind. *Charles and Lorraine might take him! They're not looking for a show dog—their clients want a pet. So he'd be perfect. And they get to choose before I do. What if . . .*

Suddenly I realized what I was doing. "God," I prayed, "there's no sense of my staying awake worrying. I choose to trust You to work this puppy situation out for Your glory."

Several times during the night I half wakened. Thoughts

jumbled in on each other. *Pick of the litter. Can't have it. What do you really want? Temperament? Looks? The Lord looks on the heart.* By about then I was awake enough to remember where I was and what was going on. "Lord," I prayed, "I choose to trust You with this. The reason I'm getting a puppy is to work for You. You know which one I need." Then rolled over and went back to sleep.

Charles and Lorraine arrived midmorning. They looked over the pups. "Joy," Lorraine said, "you're wanting a dog for a special purpose. You go ahead and choose before us."

Wonder must have shown on my face.

"Go ahead," Charles agreed.

After many thanks, I headed home with the sweetest little homely pup.

"I'm so happy you're my puppy, little guy!" I talked to him as I drove. "We'll call you Zion. Zion. I chose that name because it sounds so . . . strong and . . . majestic. And giant schnauzers always seem that way to me—big and strong and majestic. But there's another reason, too—you'll always remind me of where I'm headed—to the heavenly Zion."

The puppy cuddled beside me on a blanket.

"You're God's dog, Zion. You have a beautiful heart. You're going to help me talk to children. I don't know everything we're going to say just yet. But I think God'll help us know at the right time."

Part of the time while I drove, I sang. Sometimes I prayed. "God, I'm not sure of all the whys and wherefores, but I sense Your leading. I dedicate Zion to You, to do what You want."

At home I took Zion out of the pickup and hugged him close. He sat on my left forearm at my waist. His front paws draped over my shoulder, and he looked me in the eye.

I already felt a growing bond with my new puppy. "You're a precious pup," I told him.

Zion leaned his head forward and against the side of my face like he wanted to cuddle right there forever.

"God was right," I said. "You *are* the right one!"

When I finally stood Zion in the grass, he bounced around, sniffing and exploring his new yard with abandon.

It didn't take long to feel a bond growing.

When we went in the house, I put up puppy fences that closed the kitchen off from the rest of the house. Then I weighed Zion. Sixteen pounds.

It was a good thing Del liked animals as much as I did! For the first week or two I didn't get much accomplished other than loving the puppy. I cuddled him and pottied him and played tug-of-war and pottied him and fed him and pottied him and watered him and pottied him and played tug-of-war and . . . I took him outside every hour during the day. Or more often! At the slightest hint, whatever else was happening, we rushed outside. When he occasionally went to the door and sat down when he needed to potty, I gave him lots of praise and puppy treats.

At night Zion slept beside me in his bed on the floor. The first couple nights we made a trip outside in the middle of the night. After that, when he started to get restless I laid my hand on him or just whispered a few words, and he'd settle down. By the time Zion was 4½ months old, he sat by the door when he wanted to go outside.

Zion loved to investigate any sight, scent, or sound. When he barked about a new discovery, I'd check it out. If it was safe, I'd speak about it in a calm voice: "It's just a man walking by" or "It's just a chipmunk." My tone assured him, and he'd bound off to investigate some more in his fenced world. He loved to chase a ball or a squirrel and to play tug-of-war or most any other game in which I, his master, would spend time with him.

I made games out of commands I wanted him to learn and praised him lavishly for his accomplishments. His black eyes shone. He wagged his tail so hard he wiggled clear to his nose.

When I taught dog-training classes, I couldn't be training Zion at the same time. Also, sometimes dog trainers can be so close to their own dogs that they don't see their weaknesses or strengths. Since Zion was a special puppy with a special mission, I wanted him to have the best training possible. Besides, it felt like it was time for some fresh ideas.

I asked among dog breeders and trainers. When I was convinced Carla was the top trainer at a not-too-unreasonable distance, I drove Zion weekly from our home in Chelan, Washington, to Seattle for a puppy kindergarten class. I got tired just thinking about the drive. "Oh, well," I told Del, "it'll be three and a half hours more of bonding time going and another three and half coming home."

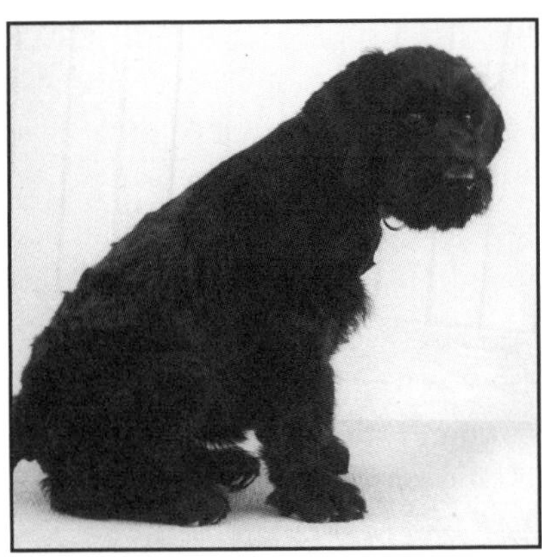

"Is he always this mellow?"

We'd barely started the first lesson when Carla pointed at Zion. "Is he always this mellow?"

"Not always," I answered.

"It concerns me," she said. "We'll have to work to get him more alert, more confident." She grabbed a rope. When it got near Zion's nose he dove for it and tugged and growled. "H'm-m-m." Carla laughed. "Maybe it won't take much work."

"One thing is very important," she told all the participants that first week. "For the first six months, don't ever let your puppy play with another dog. You want your puppy to bond to you. If they're playing and roughhousing with other dogs, they'll bond to them."

It made sense to me. And it wouldn't be any problem. Wherever I went, Zion was right on my heels.

Zion's pert little personality endeared him to me. He displayed such a sweet temperament that I tended to forget he had a face only a master could love. When I thought of *not* showing him, I felt a tinge of sadness, followed by a sense of relief. As time passed, the sadness shrank, then disappeared. The sense of relief grew to delight. Zion and I enjoyed just being puppy and master. I thanked God that I wouldn't have to bother with all the folderol that went along with showing. Zion was a quick learner. With God's blessing, we'd bless children at Vacation Bible Schools.

I could practically see Zion grow. In the first month at our house, he more than doubled his weight—from 16 pounds to 34. At 3 months, he stood 18½ inches tall at the shoulders. At 4 months, Zion weighed 40 pounds and had grown to 21 inches. At 5 months, he was 55 pounds and 23 inches at the shoulder.

Kathy phoned every week or two. "I can hardly wait to get all the puppies together. You've got to be at the show in Tacoma!"

Puppies couldn't be entered in dog shows until they were at least 6 months old. Zion would barely be eligible for the Tacoma show. Should I enter my ugly puppy in the show? It would be fun to see all Zion's littermates. And good for me to see how closely the puppies were turning out to what their early tests had indicated. I could go and see the puppies, even if I didn't show my "ugly duckling" puppy.

As the weeks passed, I thought I noticed something surprising about Zion. Could it be? *I'll just watch a few more weeks,* I thought.

Zion did well in the training class. "It's really unusual," Carla told me one day after several training sessions, "to have a dog that's so mellow and yet so alert and confident. What a wonderful combination!"

I couldn't have agreed more.

As we practiced, Zion learned a variety of commands. For starters, "come." "'Come' is one of the most important commands!" Carla emphasized. "It's basic. It can save your dog's life. Practice 'Come' till your dog will stop any activity to come to you."

Zion gets a treat for coming.

Zion also learned "Ready"—that meant, "Keep your eyes on the treat." He learned "Wait." As Zion's master, it's my job to keep him safe. When we go out a door or around a corner, we can't see what's there. So, I, his master, need to go first. When I know it's safe, then I can have him come too.

At home we practiced the commands over and over. Obeying needed to be second nature to Zion.

One evening after class I asked Carla, "How do you think Zion is developing? I mean, he started out as such a wonderful, lovable oaf of a pup."

"Well," Carla said, smiling and winking, "frankly, to me he looks a little like a miracle in installments."

My brows wrinkled.

She looked at Zion. "It seems like every week he grows a little more into those long gangly legs. Like every week he's a little better looking."

"I thought maybe it was just me thinking that."

"It's not just you, Joy. He's growing into an adorable giant."

On the way home I pondered and prayed. Should I show Zion? I wasn't surprised Kathy wanted me to show him: If he got a championship, she'd gain clout as a breeder. But Carla had nothing to gain by bragging Zion up. She knew dogs well. And she'd worked with a number of giant schnauzers.

Well, what could it hurt?

Kathy called again. "You'll be at Tacoma with Zion?" she asked.

"Planning to be there," I assured her.

Kathy rattled on about all the puppies being together. I couldn't really blame her for being so excited—this was her first litter of giant schnauzer puppies.

I registered Zion for the show. *If Zion has changed this much,* I kept wondering, *what must my first-choice puppy look like?*

For Sale?

HUNDREDS OF DOGS FILLED the Tacoma Dome. I couldn't find Kathy and her pups in the preparation areas, so Zion and I went early to the ring where giant schnauzers would be shown. No Kathy.

Fifteen minutes till their show . . . eight minutes . . . two . . .

"Giant schnauzers, puppy class," an attendant announced.

Still no Kathy. *Whatever happened?* There were no other giant schnauzer puppies. I showed Zion with older dogs. He was far too bouncy to win over the more experienced dogs. But the judge checked him over carefully. "How old is he?"

"Six months."

"Nice pup!" he said. "Give him a little time. He'll do well."

Ringside, I found Charles and Lorraine. "Where's Kathy?" I asked. "And all her puppies?"

"Haven't seen or heard a thing from her since last week," Lorraine said. "She was really excited about coming."

"Can't imagine what became of her," Charles added.

They looked Zion over and asked about him. "Nice pup," Lorraine finished. "You'll show him at spring circuit, won't you?"

"I don't know," I said. "He's s-o-o-o wiggly!"

"Another three months will make a *lot* of difference." Charles knelt down by Zion and felt his build. "He has excellent conformation, Joy. Look at his topline. See how straight his back is? It slopes just slightly up toward his head, down toward his tail. And his tail is set perfectly—right at the end of the slope."

"Yes," I responded. "That was easy to see."

"And he has a good strong prominent chest bone." Charles looked up. "Know why structure is important?"

"Because it's the basis of performance," I answered.

"Exactly," Charles agreed. "Sometimes beginners in dog showing think it's all about looks. But the structure, in other words, the conformation, is what's significant." He pointed to Zion. "Like his strong prominent chest bone," he said. "Because of that, Zion can reach far out with his front legs when he runs. So he runs with a strong fluid gait."

Charles stood up, gazing long at Zion. "He really is a beauty. He's definitely champion material!"

I knew Charles was right. Zion's conformation—his build, his structure—was excellent. But did I want to take time to show Zion? Was I willing to spend the money for registration fees and for fuel to travel with Zion?

At home Zion was a wonderful companion. I thought about introducing him to other dogs. *If it was good to keep him away from other dogs for the first six months,* I reasoned, *why change now?* Our bond grew even closer.

Zion grew in other ways, too. By 9 months he'd grown into a gorgeous giant schnauzer. He was muscular and strong. At 80 pounds and 26½ inches at the shoulders, he looked macho.

Zion cowered from nothing. When something or someone unknown approached us, a growl rumbled out of Zion's chest. Sometimes he emphasized his opinion with a deep woof. He didn't back off until I told him to. He was indeed the guard dog giant schnauzers were bred to be.

But Zion was more. He was still full of puppy wiggles and bounce. But among other dogs and people, when he was on a leash and I assured him with calmness, he responded to strangers with gentleness, even warmth.

As we headed to spring circuit—a series of eight dog shows in five towns within a few hours' drive from home—I wasn't sure if my nervousness was more from Zion's wiggles or my lack of experience.

When we arrived on the grounds of the outdoor show, dogs were everywhere on leashes or in crates—Chihuahuas and Saint Bernards, dachshunds and Great Danes, toy poodles and rottweilers. Even the other giant schnauzers didn't bother me. Only the people made me nervous.

When it came to showing, many owners handed their dogs over to professional dog handlers. The owners paid the handlers each time they showed a dog—the bigger the win, the higher the fee. The handlers made their living traveling from one show to another, showing various dogs. With their experience, they knew just what to do in the showring. In stark contrast, I was truly a novice. There was so much to learn.

I'd barely started prepping and primping Zion for the first show when Charles and Lorraine arrived. They couldn't take their eyes off Zion. "He's beautiful!" Lorraine murmured.

"More beautiful even than when we saw him at Tacoma!" Charles added.

As experienced giant schnauzer breeders and handlers they gave me some tips, and we visited while I worked.

"Have you talked to Kathy lately?" Lorraine asked.

"No," I responded. "Haven't heard from her since before the Tacoma show."

"Well, there's a reason she didn't show up."

"Yeah?"

"The pup she kept, well he didn't turn out. He has some physical problems," Lorraine said, "so he can't ever be shown."

Charles spoke up. "And he was such a beautiful pup!"

Beautiful pup? That caught my attention! *I* left *the beautiful pup!* I gazed down at Zion. *But look!*

A still small voice whispered to my mind: *"Seek ye first the kingdom of God."*

I didn't have time to give it any more thought right then.

At the first show the judge looked long at Zion, but gave the blue ribbon to an older dog.

"Nice dog," one of the professional handlers said after the judging was complete.

As we left the ring, a child about 50 feet away caught my eye. She reached out to touch a chow who'd been blow dried, brushed, and sprayed till he looked like a gold puffball. The dog's handler scowled and muttered something. The little girl jerked her hand back. Her cheeks reddened. Her mother knelt, talked to the little girl, and hugged her.

The handler stalked off, the chow following closely on his leash.

Zion followed me through the crowds till we caught up with the mother and child, now watching German shepherds in another ring. We eased in, with Zion beside the girl.

I knelt down, holding Zion's leash taut. "Would you like to pet the dog?"

The little girl's blue eyes lit up, but she leaned into her mom's leg and reached up for her hand.

The mother turned toward us. Her eyebrows raised. "Is it OK?"

"Sure," I said.

She knelt, then reached out and petted Zion's neck gently.

Zion looked at the woman and wagged his short tail.

She turned to the little girl. "It's OK if you pet this doggy."

The little girl touched Zion softly, then patted him. In a moment she was leaning into his neck and hugging him with both arms.

Zion's black eyes shone too. He leaned into her hug.

Thank You, God! I thought. *Zion will do well with the children at Vacation Bible School when he is old enough.*

But that was still a long way off—he probably wouldn't lose the puppy wiggles until he was 2 to 3 years old.

Every day at the shows dog handlers, other owners, and even judges oohed and ahhed over Zion. It was obvious I was a novice. One judge awarded Zion the blue ribbon then said, "Nice dog, but you're getting him to stretch his neck too far forward." He pointed to the dog just behind us. "See how this dog is stacked, with his head held high?"

Zion earned his first point toward championship when he was only nine months old.

I looked at how Zion stood and at how the other dog stood. "Yes, I see what you mean," I said.

"He'll look even better if you make that change."

"Thank you, sir."

The other dog's handler shot daggers my direction with her eyes. "He shows you what *I'm* doing right," she spluttered, "but gives first place to *you.*"

I swallowed hard.

The next day another handler said, "Gorgeous dog. I'd be willing to show him for you."

I'd heard about Paul. He was an excellent handler who would show only dogs he really believed in. "Thank you,"

I said, "but I can't afford to let you."

We talked a bit. When he realized how inexperienced I was and that I didn't have the money to let him or any other handler show Zion, Paul said, "He's too good a dog to let anything unnecessary hamper you. Mind if I give you a suggestion?"

"No!" I exclaimed. "I'd appreciate it!"

Paul showed me how to improve the way Zion and I ran together in the ring. He helped me understand and practice the better technique. It really would help a judge see Zion's fast fluid movement which was only possible because he was exceptionally well built. Before he left, Paul said, "He's a beautiful dog! You're going to get lots of opportunities with him. Please feel free to ask me questions if there's anything I can help you with. Anytime."

I marveled at Paul's kindness. There were no cash prizes in dog showing. Even though if Zion won, it would cut into his and the other handlers' earnings and prestige, Paul was still willing to share his knowledge. *God,* I prayed, *help me be that kind, that generous.*

On Friday Kathy watched the show with Charles and Lorraine. Afterward she gushed over Zion and his new blue ribbon.

"Well," Lorraine said eventually, "I've gotta go. Nice to see you, Kathy. See you tomorrow, Joy."

"Yeah," Kathy said. "Good to see you."

"We won't be at tomorrow's show," I replied. "But we'll see you Sunday."

Surprise crossed Kathy's, Lorraine's, and Charles' faces. "What's going on tomorrow?" Lorraine asked.

"I'll be in church."

"Church?" all three questioned practically together.

After an instant of shocked silence, Lorraine asked, "What time is church? Could you make the show first?"

I grinned. "No, no. It's God's Sabbath, and I'll spend the day with Him."

Kathy spoke up. "But you'll show Zion on Saturdays later, won't you?"

"No."

Kathy's mouth dropped open. "Most of the shows are on Saturday and Sunday. He'll never go anyplace if you don't show him on Saturday!"

"I'll leave that up to God," I said.

"But you have to show him!" she insisted. "You have the only dog out of the whole litter that turned out to be a show dog. And he's a beauty. You *have* to show him!"

"Any day but Saturdays," I responded.

She threw her hands in the air. "A true champion, and he'll never go anyplace!" She was still shaking her head as she turned to leave. "What a waste!" she muttered.

On Sunday Zion took the blue ribbon in puppy class and went on to compete with more mature dogs. After each dog had gone through its paces, the judge pointed at Zion. "First," she announced. She motioned us to move to the winner lineup.

I hesitated. *Did I hear what I think I heard?*

The judge motioned again.

We moved to the winner line.

Eager to learn all I could, as the ring cleared I asked the judge, "With all the more mature and experienced giants, why did you put him up?"

"He's the better dog," she answered matter-of-factly.

Ringside, Charles and Lorraine grinned from ear to ear. Charles scratched Zion's ears and patted his side. "Congratulations, big guy! Ya did good! Really, really good!"

"Joy," Lorraine asked, "do you realize what you have in this dog?" Wonder was written all over her face. She looked and motioned toward Zion. "He's only 9 months old. Still a puppy! And he's already won a point toward championship!" For a moment she feasted her eyes on Zion in silence. Finally she added, "He's incredible!"

We'd barely said our goodbyes and turned to leave when a stranger approached. I'd noticed her occasionally at this circuit of shows, but I knew nothing about her. "I need to talk to you about your dog. Could we go where it's quieter?"

Zion and I followed, zigzagging through the crowd of people and dogs. Under the awning of a luxurious motor home the woman turned, and held out her diamond-studded hand. "I'm Mae Lewis," she introduced herself. "I want a giant schnauzer. I've asked all the handlers, 'What's the best giant out there?' Everybody said, 'Zion.' Everybody!" She hesitated an instant, then dropped her bombshell. "I'd like to buy him."

I blinked, recovering from the surprise. "He's not for sale."

"Money isn't an issue," she said. "How much would you like for him?"

"He's not for sale," I repeated. "He's going to help me teach children about God when—"

Mae Lewis waved her hand to silence me. "You're not talking sense." She shook her head. "Whatever you're talking about, some other dog can do that. *Zion's* a show dog!" She paused and looked me straight in the eye. "Name the price. Any amount."

I looked down at Zion. *He could really go places if he belonged to someone with money enough for the best groomers and the best handlers. Someone who'd show him more than I ever could. Would it be selfish for me to keep him?*

CHAPTER 6

Surprise

MY THOUGHTS WHIRLED. *Of course Zion could really go places if he had more financial backing than I could give him. But he's my dog, and I love him . . . No! He's God's dog. Maybe this is God's way of helping us get out of debt. To get a car that doesn't have 200,000 miles on it. God gave me one dog. He could give me another good dog.*

Mae Lewis broke the silence. "Think about it," she said. She turned and stepped into her motor home.

My legs felt like spaghetti.

As I drove toward home a tempest of thoughts crashed against each other.

Should I sell Zion? Sure, I had a dream of Zion and me teaching children spiritual lessons. But there isn't any assurance it will work. It didn't with Casey.

The familiar Bible verse came to mind: *"But seek ye first the kingdom of God, and his righteousness; and all these things shall be added unto you" (Matthew 6:33, KJV).*

"God," I said aloud, "I want Your kingdom first."

The engine hummed. I reached over and patted Zion. He shifted, then laid a front paw on my leg.

"O God, how could I let him go?" A tear slid down my cheek. A few minutes later I added, "And God, if I keep Zion, should I keep showing him?"

I felt an obligation toward Charles and Lorraine. After all, out of Zion's litter they were supposed to have chosen before me. But they knew I wanted a special dog for a special purpose, and they let me have the puppy I wanted. Also, they hadn't been blinded by money and prestige in the dog world. They truly loved giant schnauzers and carefully bred for good temperament and health as well as for beauty. I just couldn't let them down.

As for Mae Lewis's offer, well, who was she anyway? Did she have money enough that her offer really meant anything?

Over the next few weeks I showed Zion several more times. At every show he won a blue ribbon in his first competition.

At each show Zion's first competition was against other giant schnauzers in his class. For each breed there were six classes of males and six of females—puppy, 12-18 months—and four classes for adult dogs: novice, bred by exhibitor, American-bred, and open class. The blue-ribbon winners in each class then competed against each other. Only the winners of this competition—one male and one female of each breed—received points toward championship.

To become a champion, Zion would need 15 points. The number of points he received with each win depended on the number of dogs he won over. Though it was unusual for the

Winning takes work: practice, practice, practice.

same dog to win points repeatedly, for several weeks Zion earned points toward championship at each show.

Should I keep showing Zion and try to make him a champion? I wondered. Every show still made my heart throb and my knees knock.

I have to, I thought, *for Charles and Lorraine. Besides, as much as he's winning, it won't take long. A few more shows; then I'll stay home with Del.*

Sometimes Del went to the shows with Zion and me; sometimes he couldn't. As a laboratory and X-ray technologist he had to take his turn on call. He didn't complain about my absences, and he always wanted to know how the competitions had gone. But I preferred the trips when Del went along.

Several times at various shows I saw Mae Lewis ringside watching Zion. After a show one morning I asked another handler, "Do you know anything about Mae Lewis?"

He looked up. His eyes glanced around the ring we'd just left, then back to me. "The lady in the fur coat on the north side of the ring?" he asked.

I glanced that direction. "Yeah."

"Not much," he answered. "Just that she loves dogs and recently was given $30 million. Rumor has it that she's keeping her eye out for a few really good dogs and that she especially likes giant schnauzers. Have you noticed her eyeing your dog?"

"Yes."

He motioned toward Zion. "I noticed her a couple times this last show," he said. "She had her eyes glued on him."

Interesting. Zion and I headed for home.

Late one evening the phone rang. "Joy, you've got to help me."

"What do you need?"

"I know you told me Zion wouldn't be ready till next year," the Vacation Bible School leader said. "But the woman who had

Wednesday's special feature had to leave town on an emergency."

I drew in a deep breath.

"You and Zion can do something, can't you?" she pleaded. "Just *one* time?"

"Zion's still a bouncy pup," I hedged. I sent an SOS heavenward, *Lord, what should I do?* My mind whirled. Would it even be safe to take an 80-pound dog that wasn't well trained into a group of children?

"The kids loved Casey so much last year!" the leader said. "It would be really special for them."

I remembered the kids' excitement when they saw the dog. And the delight that sparked the children's chanting, "Ca-sey! Ca-sey! Ca-sey!" But what could Zion and I do? He responded to "Come" and "Down." I could keep him on a leash. He was pretty good about not pulling too hard on his leash. If he lay down when the children came to pet him, he wouldn't accidentally knock some kid over or fall like a ton of bricks on top of one. He was pretty mellow when we met people. And this was why God gave me a dog. Or was it? Finding out how Zion worked with children might help me decide once and for all about Mae Lewis's offer. Was it time to try Vacation Bible School?

"Yes," I heard myself say. "I think we can do *something.*"

"Well, Lord," I said as the receiver clicked into place, "I didn't think we were ready yet. Sort of seems like You have a different idea. You and I both know we'll need Your help! So what do we do Wednesday?"

A couple ideas came. Zion and I prepared as much as we could in three days. Over and over I reminded myself that God had picked Zion. I felt excitement . . . and dread.

We worked especially hard on "Settle." It was a calming command. It meant for Zion to just be quiet and calm. I was glad then that he'd started learning "Settle" months before.

Tuesday afternoon I bathed Zion and readied him as if he

were going to the prestigious Westminster Dog Show at Madison Square Garden in New York City. We were, after all, on a special mission.

Wednesday morning I gave Zion a final brushing, then got out his collar and leash. I stood back and looked. My heart beat a little faster. "Thank You, God," I whispered. "He's beautiful!" Tears came to my eyes. "He's Yours, God. And I'm Yours. Please help us."

I thought about the children again. Zion was so tall that if he and a child were standing toe to toe, in many cases they'd be nose to nose. Would he frighten them?

I got a red bandanna and tied it around Zion's neck. I stood back again. *Yeah. That softens him. He doesn't look quite so daunting.*

As we climbed into the car, my heart pounded in my temples. "God," I prayed, "Vacation Bible School is the whole reason I got Zion. Please help us. Please don't let him hurt a child. Please use us!"

At the church we waited in a side room while the children gathered. Zion's ears turned toward the sounds from the sanctuary. He started to get up.

"Zion."

He turned toward me.

"Down."

He lay back down.

"Go-o-d. Go-o-d."

Zion lay there, with encouragement. But his ears, twitching toward different sounds, alerted me that he was curious about what was going on in the next room.

Then I heard the leader say, "Boys and girls, what did I promise you for today?"

"Surprise!" a chorus of children's voices answered.

Zion's head snapped toward the sound. Instantly, he was on all fours. A ferocious rumble was sure to follow.

CHAPTER 7

Showtime

MY HEART RACED. "Zion, settle," I said instantaneously, forcing my voice to stay soft.

Standing at full attention, Zion turned his head toward me, then snapped it back toward the door.

"It's just children, Zion," I said in the same calm voice that I'd so often used when he got excited about a squirrel or a bird. "It'll be fine. It's just some children."

His head relaxed but stayed alert. He looked at me again.

"Zion, settle," I said in a soothing voice. "Go-o-d. Go-o-d."

"Yes," the leader said. "Joy Matthews came today, and she has a special surprise for us."

"This is it, Lord," I whispered. "Please use us."

Zion and I walked out onto the platform at the front of the sanctuary. The children gasped. I held Zion's leash tightly. He walked beside me, looking into the sea of children's faces.

When I introduced Zion, the children's eyes sparkled. Those in the back craned their necks to get a better view.

Zion sat beside me, surveying the audience. His ears turned when a child squirmed to see better or scuffed a shoe or cleared their throat.

"Jesus taught me how to treat Zion," I said. "Jesus is always kind. The Bible says that Jesus wants me to come to Him. And He draws me with loving-kindness [Jeremiah 31:3]." I talked about Jesus' kindness, then asked, "Do you like people who treat you kindly?"

"Yes," a hundred children chorused.

Zion's ears perked up again.

"Animals like us when we are kind to them, too. How can we be kind to our animals?"

"Pet them," a towheaded boy on the front row said.

"Yes," I responded. "How can I pet Zion kindly? By stroking him gently." I demonstrated with my hand. "And Zion likes it," I said, lowering my voice to a near whisper, "when I speak to him with a soft, gentle voice."

Soon I moved away from Zion and asked him to come, then to sit. He followed my commands like he was a pro.

At the end I sent a silent SOS heavenward. *God, do I dare let all these kids pet him?*

It's time, I sensed.

"Zion, down," I said. Zion lay down. "Zion, stay." I knelt beside him and grasped his leash with a bulldog grip. I looked out over rows of rambunctious children and took a deep breath. "OK, kids. Now you can come pet Zion."

I looked back down at Zion and locked my eyes on him. A hundred children's feet landed on the floor and charged toward us. My heart raced. My palms turned cold and clammy. I tightened my death grip on Zion's leash.

Either this would work . . . or it wouldn't.

Suddenly Zion and I were surrounded. Eight-year-olds, 4-year-olds, 12-year-olds, and others in between came at him from every direction. Those closest smothered him with petting and patting. Zion looked into the eyes of one child and then another as if to say, "Wow! This is great! Thank you for coming."

The children kept coming and kept petting and patting and oohing and ahhing. Zion kept calmly looking from one child to another.

And my heart shouted to heaven! *Thank You, God! Thank You! Thank You!*

When the children were gone, I petted and patted Zion too. "You were wonderful, Zion!" I enthused. His stubby tail wiggled back and forth. With tears of joy I buried my face in his neck and hugged him and stroked his soft side.

"God," I prayed, "Thank You *so* much! This *was* Your idea, wasn't it? You chose Zion. You turned the ugly pup into a gorgeous dog. You gave him a temperament just perfect for doing Your work with Your kids. He's Your dog! Teach me what You want from me."

Just keep seeking Me. I have plans, plans that are just right for Zion—and for you.

His last phrase caught me off guard. But I sensed assurance. "Thank You, God," I whispered.

Eager to finish getting Zion's championship so I could forget showing and concentrate on sharing with children, I headed to the next show.

Mae Lewis caught up with us right after Zion's first showing and another blue ribbon. "Good morning." She looked down at Zion and patted his head. "How's my big boy?"

I swallowed hard. "Good morning."

"Well." She looked up. "How much is it going to take to make this dog mine?"

"He's still not for sale," I said.

She reached out and touched my hand. "You obviously love your dog," she said. "I'll treat him well—the best care, the best handlers. I've noticed he's missed some shows. I'll take him to all the best shows. I'll make you proud!"

I shook my head. "No, Ms. Lewis. He's God's dog. He's not mine to sell."

Her smile disappeared. Her eyes narrowed. "I realize he is a very good dog. And he won't be cheap. I'm willing to pay top dollar."

It would be nice to get ahead financially, to get a car . . . I stopped the mental tape midsentence. "I appreciate that, Ms. Lewis. But he's not for sale. There are some things that no amount of money can buy."

Mae Lewis's expression turned gray. Silence hung between us. "Well . . ." She cleared her throat. She looked down at Zion, then returned her gaze to meet mine. "If you change your mind, I'll be around."

Next time in the ring Zion won another point toward championship.

"At the rate Zion's going," Lorraine enthused, "he'll get his championship in no time. Then you can special him. He has such wonderful potential!"

A sick feeling thudded into the pit of my stomach. "Special him?"

"Yes. You know. Keep showing him against the champions. The more he wins, the more prestige he gets, and the more prestige you get as a giant schnauzer owner and handler, and the more money you can make someday with stud fees or with raising pups."

I grinned. "And the more clout you get as a breeder?"

"Well, yeah." She nodded and smiled. "That too."

On the way home, my stomach felt like I'd swallowed a rock the size of Grand Coulee Dam. "God," I prayed, "I thought if I showed Zion till he earned championship, I'd be through with showing. That I would have met the obligation I felt to Charles and Lorraine. Isn't that enough? What do You want?"

All I heard was the drone of the engine.

At practically every show I asked Paul, the extra-helpful handler, another question or three—sometimes about Zion, sometimes about what to do in the ring. Paul always happily answered whatever question I asked.

At every show, Zion won. Over and over I thanked God

for the kind judges, handlers, and owners who helped me learn along the way. My knees didn't knock so much anymore when I took Zion into the ring. In fact, I began looking at the other Giants as we lined up before a show. *Bad grooming . . . Poor topline . . . Not under control very well . . . No question,* I'd think, *Zion will win this one.*

The winning—the prestige—felt good. *Maybe Zion and I do belong in showing,* I began thinking.

The more time I spent training, grooming, and showing Zion, the less time I had for everything else—including horses. It seemed Del and I hardly got to ride anymore. When a family who could give the horses the time and love they needed asked to buy them, we agreed.

Letting Shannon go was especially hard. It would have been a thousand times worse if I hadn't known I could visit her anytime I wanted to. To fill the empty spot in my heart, I put all the more energy into Zion.

Joyce encouraged me to show Zion every chance I got. She was another giant schnauzer owner who showed her own dog and understood how tough it was for a novice to gain respect. Talking on the phone a few days before one of the bigger shows in the Northwest, she asked, "You'll have Zion at both shows, won't you?"

"We'll be at the Sunday show," I said. "But not Saturday. I never show on Saturday."

"I know," she replied. "But this is a bigger show. If you'd show Zion Saturday, he might even finish his championship."

"We'll do what we can on the other days," I said. "Besides, my husband will be with me at the show in Boise, Idaho. If Zion gets his championship there, Del can see him too and videotape it."

"But this would be a chance for Zion to get major points," Joyce said.

No matter how many single points a dog won, to earn

championship it had to win two majors. A dog won a major when it won at least three points in a single competition. Often at the smaller shows only one or two points were possible. "God will help us get majors in the right time," I said.

I didn't show Zion Saturday. But as usual, my thoughts kept wandering to dog showing. I pulled my mind back to the Sabbath School discussion, the sermon, or the book I was reading.

On Sunday Zion won his first three-point major.

A few weeks later at a show at Eugene, Oregon, Zion placed second on Thursday. One of his competitors who didn't place was a scruffy-looking giant with a professional handler from outside the Northwest. The handler obviously wasn't used to losing. When we left the ring, he eyed Zion with a look that said, "Where'd this dog come from?"

On Friday the same dog was being shown by a better-known handler with more clout. In the end the judge pointed to Zion. "Winner." The handler of the scruffy giant glared daggers at me. As she passed us, she glanced at Zion and spat words just loud enough for me to hear: "Not this again!" She stomped out of the ring with the dog.

What was that all about? I wondered as we left the ring. But I didn't have time to worry about it then. Zion had just earned three points, the last major he needed. All that was left for his championship was two points. A thrill tingled down my spine. Now he was in a good position to finish at Boise, where Del could be with me.

Immediately we went to compete for Best of Breed. Three dogs were in the ring: Zion, who was not even a champion yet, and two seasoned champions who had each been specialed and had won many honors. I grinned at the foolishness of even being there. *Oh well,* I thought, *experience never hurts.*

Zion and I ran our paces along with the other dogs. The

judge examined Zion just as he did the champions. He stepped back and glanced over all three dogs again. "Around the ring again," he said. As soon as we all stopped, the judge pointed directly to Zion. "Best of Breed."

My mouth dropped open. I stood there in shock. At 15 months my "pup" had just won Best of Breed over champion giant schnauzers.

I blinked a couple times, trying to grasp the magnitude of Zion's win. Suddenly another thought blasted into my mind. Zion had just won two more points. Besides winning Best of Breed, at 15 months, Zion had also earned the title of American Kennel Club Champion.

Ringside, Lorraine ended her congratulations with "What were you thinking in there? You had the weirdest look on your face."

"Well," I said, "I was thinking, 'Why, Lord?'" Shaking my head, I added, "This sure wasn't the way I had things planned. I never dreamed of a win this big!"

"It's a tremendous win!" Lorraine said. She glanced at her watch. "Two more hours and . . ." She reached down and patted Zion. ". . . and Zion goes into his first working group competition."

My heart raced, and my mind whirled. American Kennel Club recognized seven groups of dogs—sporting, hound, working, terrier, toy, nonsporting, and herding. Group competitions were between the Best of Breed dog of each breed in that group. Zion would compete in the working group along with Doberman Pinschers, Great Danes, rottweilers, Saint Bernards, Siberian huskies, and several other breeds.

I'd planned to prepare myself for group showing when the possibility neared. Suddenly there was no time for preparation. My stomach felt so nervous that I thought it best to skip lunch. I brushed Zion and answered some admirers' questions. The two hours seemed like a forever that raced by in an instant.

Heart still pounding, I entered the working group ring. The handler who'd spat the words "Not this again!" took her place with a Samoyed right behind Zion and me in the line. But her dog acted out of control. He bounced around, nearly bumping Zion several times. And the handler egged him on rather than stopping him.

Zion stood tall, ears alert. I calmed him as best I could, trying to keep as much space as possible between the two dogs. But I couldn't move forward. The Husky ahead of Zion jumped around also. It even turned around and jumped at Zion.

I had never seen dogs act so out of control in the ring.

The handler ahead glanced back surreptitiously a couple times at the handler behind Zion and me. The dog behind nearly ran into Zion again. Zion gave a low, "back off" growl.

"Come"

FINALLY, THE JUDGE GOT THE SHOW on the road. I haven't the foggiest idea who won. I was just glad to get Zion out of there.

After the show, as happened so often, children petted Zion. He leaned into their hugs. Another handler who'd been friendly in the past joined us. "What was going on in the ring this last show?" he asked.

"I don't know," I said. "Is working group usually like that?"

"No! In 15 years as a handler I've never seen two dogs so out of control!"

"Do you know anything about the handler who was ahead of Zion?" I asked.

"She usually shows sporting dogs," he said. "I've never seen her in the working group before. Maybe her business partner had two dogs she needed to show at the same time."

"Business partner? Who's her business partner?"

"The woman who was right behind you in the lineup."

"Really?"

"Yeah. She's something. Has lots of money behind her. Gets as friendly as she can with the judges. Does a lot of winning. In fact, she expects to win because she's who she is, whether or not the dog she shows is any good."

I didn't like the way the pieces of the puzzle were fitting

Zion and I competing in the Working Group.

together. The more I thought about it the next couple weeks, the more frustrated I got. It was true—the professional handlers lost money every time Zion won. And I suppose it was hard on their pride when a novice showed his or her own dog and won.

But, these are dog shows, aren't they? I stewed. *Not handler shows.* I wanted reality to fit my idealistic picture: All judges are fair. All handlers have good motives. And the best dog always wins.

Sure, I liked it when Zion won. But if he wasn't the best, the one who was should win.

Zion had his championship. I was tempted to scrap dog showing. But he was already signed up for the Boise show. And Del's mom lived in the area so we'd get to visit her. We might as well go. Besides, maybe the Boise shows would restore my confidence in dog shows and the people involved.

On Sabbath at Boise, Zion rested, and Del and I went to a nearby church. That morning, when the pastor invited children forward for a story, a small voice whispered to my mind, "You and Zion could tell children's stories in the different churches you visit."

It felt like a lightbulb switched on in my brain. It made perfect sense. A children's story for church wouldn't be much different than a feature for Vacation Bible School. And wherever we traveled for dog shows, on Sabbath I went to a local church. But I was a lot more comfortable in front of an audience of children than I was in front of their parents. And what would people think of a dog in church?

God, if this is Your idea, I prayed silently, *I'm willing to try. But You'll have to work it out and help me know what to say.*

That afternoon a group from the church planned to visit a nursing home. "We'd love to have you join us," a man invited.

I hesitated a moment. "We have a giant schnauzer show dog in our travel trailer," I said. "I hate to leave him there by himself all day. He's well behaved. Do you think anyone would mind if we took him in?"

"I think the people would love it!" he responded. "Bring him along."

At the nursing home Zion sat quietly beside me as the group sang. Afterward the visitors greeted the residents. When I approached a white-haired man, I asked, "Would you like to pet my dog?"

The elderly man looked up at me with tired eyes, then down at Zion. He slid an unsteady hand forward and reached for Zion's head. Zion moved closer and looked into the man's eyes.

A smile lit up the man's weathered face. His eyes danced. He stroked Zion's head and neck.

I stood mesmerized. I hadn't trained Zion to look people in the eye. But he did it at Vacation Bible School, with one child and then another. Now he looked this stranger in the eye, as if to say, "Hi. You're the most important person in the world. How are you?"

"What's his name?" the man asked, pulling me out of my spellbound wonder.

"Zion."

"Zion," he said, looking into the dog's eyes. "You're a handsome fellow, and soft as the goose down I used to help my mother stuff pillows with when I was a young'un. . . . Way back then we had a black dog. . . . His name was King."

The man stroked or patted Zion as he wove his words. I felt almost like I was eavesdropping on a private conversation.

Soon a nursing assistant came to get the man for supper. The elderly man shot me a smile that lit up the room. "Thank you, lady, for bringing your dog! He's a *real* good listener." The man gave Zion a final pat. "This is the best day I've had in a good long time!"

My heart beat fast. A smile welled up inside me. In my journal that evening I wrote, "It was a great day for me, too."

Sunday morning Zion placed first—a prestigious win. He won over the giant schnauzer who had just won Best of Breed at Westminster.

That dog's handler stopped me outside the ring. "Nice dog!" he said. "Mind if I take a look at him?"

"Fine," I said. He knelt and examined Zion. He was a fair and very accomplished handler. In fact, he had also just taken a Dalmatian to Best in Show at Westminster—the most prestigious honor at the most prestigious dog show in the United States.

"You'd better get prepared, lady," he finally said.

Question must have been written all over my face.

"You're going to get a lot of opportunities," he said. "He's an all-around champion. He's going to do a lot of winning!"

Maybe, I thought, *if some crazy handler doesn't ruin him first.*

At home in our fenced yard, I practiced obedience commands with Zion every day. He knew "Circle," "Back," and "Go around me." It was fun to watch him learn new things. But we kept practicing the old lessons, too. We practiced one particular command over and over—"Come."

Now, even when he started to chase a squirrel, if I called,

"Zion, come," he'd wheel around and race to me. *Will he respond as quickly if he ever faces a dangerous situation?* I wondered occasionally.

One day as we practiced, a new concept flashed into my mind. Then I heard God whisper, *That would make a good children's story for church.*

I hadn't given children's stories any more thought since the idea first popped into my mind. "God," I prayed, "is that really something I should pursue?"

Yes.

"Would it be OK to take a dog to church?"

Yes.

"But how would people know to ask me?"

Don't you have a telephone?

"You mean offer?"

Sure.

"You'll have to help me."

Immediately Scripture verses I had memorized came to my mind: *"So do not fear, for I am with you; do not be dismayed, for I am your God. I will strengthen you and help you; I will uphold you with my righteous right hand"* (Isaiah 41:10). *"And, lo, I am with you alway, even unto the end of the world"* (Matthew 28:20, KJV).

When I went back into the house, I wrote the story idea in my journal. A few weeks before the next show, I telephoned the pastor of a church in that area. I didn't know what to expect. *Oh well, they can't do anything worse than say no.*

"I have a champion giant schnauzer that I'll be showing at the dog show in your area," I told the pastor. "He and I helped with Vacation Bible School last summer. He's very well mannered. And I'd be willing to tell the children's story on the Sabbath that we're there, using the dog to illustrate a lesson."

I expected questions about the idea of a dog in church. What I heard was: "Which week was that?" and "Yes, we'd be delighted to have you and your dog tell the story that day!"

"OK, God," I prayed as I hung up the phone, "now You need to help me put it together and then help me tell it."

On that Sabbath morning, I introduced Zion to the children, then asked, "What's the most important thing I can teach my dog?"

"No!" shouted a small boy.

I said, "that's not it. No, think again. What's the most important word I could teach my dog, Zion?"

The kids came up with "Sit," and "Speak," and "Roll over."

Vavra Photography

"Zion, front."

"Let's let Zion show you what the most important word is," I said. I had Zion sit and stay. Then I walked across the room. "Zion," I said, "come."

Zion stood, walked straight to me, and sat in front of me, looking straight up into my face.

"Come is the most important thing I can teach Zion to do," I said. "If Zion will always obey when I say 'Come,' I can protect him from danger. If Zion comes when I call him, we get to spend special time together. We may go for a walk, or play tug-the-rope, or chase-the-ball."

The children listened with rapt attention.

"Jesus taught me a very important lesson," I finished. "The most important thing that boys and girls and moms and dads and grandmas and grandpas can do, is also to come—to come to

Jesus. When we come to Jesus, He can protect us from many dangers. When we come to Jesus every day, Jesus can do special things with us."

As I finished, I invited the children to pet Zion. Again they mobbed him. Again he looked into the eyes of each child one at a time. His tail wagged with each child's petting.

After the church service one girl about 8 years old, came to me. "I'm going to come to Jesus every day," she said, "just like Zion comes to you when you call him. And like my dog comes to me."

A thrill coursed up my spine. Now whenever this child called her dog, she'd be reminded to come to Jesus.

Thank You, God! Please keep this little girl coming to You! Thank You for using Zion and me.

Just Once?

THE NEXT MORNING AT THE DOG SHOW Zion won over all the other giant schnauzers to earn Best of Breed.

Showing gave us a reason for being in different areas where Zion and I could tell children's stories. The first time we were invited back to tell a second story, I wasn't sure what to do. *Go ahead,* I heard God nudge.

I accepted the invitation, then started praying. A couple weeks before the story, a thought flashed through my mind. Zion almost always obeyed better if he was looking at me when I gave a command. And I obey God better if I'm focused on Him.

Zion had already learned to snap his attention to me when I said, "Zion, watch." With a little more practice, we had another story. It was a good thing—over the next nine months we traveled to 20 different shows and told the second story in each of those 20 churches.

Often on Sabbath mornings when I pulled Zion's bandanna out of the drawer, he jumped up and bounced over to me. He stood still, his stub tail wagging, while I tied the bandanna around his neck. Then he sat by the door until we left for church.

Zion never showed such eagerness when we headed for a dog show. But he knew a bandanna signaled time with children.

I loved watching Zion's response to children and children's responses to him. But during the sermon or during Sabbath afternoon I'd suddenly realize my mind was at a dog show. Sometimes I was reliving a victory, sometimes trying to figure out what to do about the one thing that marred my excitement about showing—lately, sometimes, Zion would "talk" in the showring. The sound he made wasn't really a growl. More like a grumble. A throaty warning to another dog who got too close: "I'm a guard dog. Please don't push me." It didn't happen often, but it bothered me when it did.

Vavra Photography

"Zion, watch."

At those 20 shows Zion went undefeated, racking up 20 Best of Breed ribbons. Visions of fame and fortune danced in my mind. At home we continually practiced obedience commands and showmanship. In shows Zion began winning in the working group over dogs of different breeds. I was proud of Zion . . . and proud of myself. Dog showing began taking over my thinking, my life.

In the midst of all Zion's winnings, my biggest concern was his "grumbling." As I thought about it, I realized it had started since the two dogs had riled him up in the ring.

Starting in April a second issue vied for "most frustrating."

"You'll be at Nationals in July, won't you?" Lorraine asked at a Thursday show in Spring Circuit.

"What's Nationals?" I responded.

"Nationals is the biggest, most prestigious show of the year

Zion winning in the working group. His success began taking over my life.

for any breed," Lorraine explained. "This Nationals will be where all the best giant schnauzers from all over the nation come. And this year, with Zion just coming into his prime, it will be really close for you. It's near Vancouver, Washington."

"Sounds interesting," I said. "When is it?"

"Second Saturday in July."

"Any other days?" I asked.

"There'll be Regionals on Sunday and Monday," she answered. "But Nationals is only one show every year."

"Oh. Too bad it's on Saturday," I said. "As you know, we don't show on Saturday." In my mind, that was the end of that.

Lorraine's eyebrows scrunched toward each other. She shook her head in disbelief. "I know you don't ordinarily show on Saturday, but Nationals is no ordinary show!"

The next day Zion won another Best of Breed. I was glad it was Friday—I was exhausted and ready for a rest day. As we headed for our trailer, Charles and Lorraine caught up with us. "Good job!" Charles congratulated.

"Zion's doing so well!" Lorraine enthused.

"Thanks, guys." I appreciated the help and support Charles and Lorraine had been in the past. They'd become special friends.

"So well," Lorraine continued, "that he just might do some winning at Nationals." She smiled enticingly as she spoke, then looked longingly at Zion.

"Yeah," I responded. "I wish it were a different day."

"But you won't let the day stop you from Nationals, will you?" Lorraine countered.

"We simply don't show on Saturday at any show."

"But—" Lorraine sighed. "But why?"

"Because, as I understand the Bible, it's the day God chose as a special day for us to spend with Him. It's—"

Lorraine jumped in. "We've tried to understand. We've never asked you to show Zion any other Saturday. But this is Nationals!" She gestured with her arms as she talked. "And it's perfect for Zion! The first time he's old enough to compete in Nationals, and it's practically in your backyard!" Lorraine hardly stopped for a breath. "And Zion's on a winning streak. He's an up-and-coming giant. And Nationals won't be in the West for another four years! This is your opportunity to have Zion seen! To start making some money."

I was beginning to feel like a strand of spaghetti that had boiled for an hour. "I'm sorry to disappoint you," I said, "but, no, I won't show him *any* Saturday."

The furrows in Lorraine's forehead deepened.

"I've really got to be going now," I said. "A friend's expecting me. Will I see you guys at the Sunday show?"

Lorraine didn't seem to notice my question. "Can't you show him just once?"

"I really have to go," I said and started to walk away.

Lorraine sighed.

When Zion and I had walked about 20 feet, she ran after us

and walked beside me. She badgered me all the way to our trailer.

"You *have* to show him!" she insisted just before I stepped inside. "In 25 years of breeding giant schnauzers, he's the best dog we've *ever* produced!"

Inside I collapsed onto the bed. My head pounded. Lorraine was my friend. The pressure felt like a vice squeezing tighter and tighter till I could barely breathe.

"God . . ." Words wouldn't even come.

Suddenly, in the midst of my mental fog, a sentence stood out clearly in my mind: "The world and it's desires pass away, but the man who does the will of God lives forever."

My mind began to focus. I realized that was a verse from the Bible. I had read it sometime—1 John 2:17.

Trophies, ribbons, and titles will pass away, I thought. *Even the pressure and desire to compromise principle will pass away. But if I choose the will of God, that decision will send happy ripples through eternity.*

I repeated the verse.

This situation isn't exactly a biggie, I thought. *Some people have given their lives for what they believe.* I lay there, staring at the bottom of the top bunk.

"But Jesus," I said, "she's my friend. This pressure hurts. It feels *so* horrid!"

It Would Only Be Fair

I SENSED JESUS UNDERSTOOD about disappointing friends. "I'm doing what I understand is right," I said.

Even while I ached because I was disappointing my friends, I felt gentle comfort from my Forever Friend.

I sat up on the edge of the bed and pressed my temples. The headache eased slightly. I really did need to go, before my friend sent out a search party.

In the van Zion sat in the passenger seat, oblivious to the firestorm he'd set off. When we arrived at my friend's house, she didn't even say hello. She took one look at me and said, "You need a hug!"

Her hug bolstered my courage.

"What's going on?" she questioned.

I shared. God used this friend to strengthen me over that Sabbath.

Saturday evening I drove three hours to the next show grounds. I hoped I'd made my position clear enough to Charles and Lorraine that I'd hear no more about showing Zion at Nationals.

Sunday morning as I prepped Zion, I saw Lorraine coming. Ordinarily, I would have been delighted. This time dread settled over me.

"Joy," she started, "I really hope you've reconsidered.

Nationals is so significant to a dog's success."

The encounter dragged on. When it was clear I wouldn't waver, Lorraine countered with "If you're not going to show Zion, how about letting someone else show him?"

That caught me by surprise. "I'll have to think about that," I responded.

"It would only be fair to him," she added. "And to us!"

That barb pricked at my conscience. Charles and Lorraine had helped me in many ways. They were my friends. It hurt to disappoint them. Might it be all right to let someone else show Zion on Sabbath?

I had a hard time focusing my attention on the show that morning. In spite of me, Zion got another Best of Breed.

At home I puzzled over the question of letting someone else show Zion on Sabbath. I studied the Bible. I prayed. I talked with friends, with my pastor. One day I decided no. The next day I changed it to yes. An hour later I didn't know. For days I vacillated.

One morning, my Bible open, I desperately threw the dilemma before God. "I've got to give them an answer. I want to do right. But I don't know what to do. You promised wisdom. *Please* help me!"

I don't know how I ended up in Deuteronomy 5. But I read the Sabbath commandment. Then I thought back. *God changed Zion from a scruffy pup to a head-turning champion. God gave him a perfect temperament to minister. God arranged for amazing winnings—even with a novice owner/handler.* I realized anew, *He truly is God's dog!* Conviction grew: *I don't think God wants His dog working on His special day.*

"But how do I answer Charles and Lorraine?" I asked God. "When I quote the commandment, she says, 'Zion's not a cattle'" (the word used in Deuteronomy 5:14, KJV).

For some reason I turned to the same text in my New

International Version: "Observe the Sabbath day by keeping it holy, as the Lord your God has commanded you. Six days you shall labor and do all your work, but the seventh day is a Sabbath to the Lord your God. On it you shall not do any work, neither you, nor your son or daughter, nor your manservant or maidservant, nor your ox, your donkey or any of your animals" (verses 12-14).

My eyes—and mind—locked onto that last phrase, "or any of your animals." Instantly, I knew.

"Thank You, God! Now, please give me the strength."

I telephoned right away. "Lorraine, I respect you and Charles. I like you guys. And it feels awful to disappoint you . . ." I took a big breath. "But I can't let Zion be shown on God's Sabbath."

Lorraine's voice dripped disappointment.

Kathy telephoned occasionally and poured on the pressure.

Ten days before Nationals, Lorraine telephoned again. "Joy, you know what I want. *Please,* just this once?" she pleaded. "Just once."

"Lorraine," I asked, "have you seen the movie *Chariots of Fire?"*

"I-I-I think so."

"Remember when Eric Liddell was getting so much pressure for not running on what he believed was God's day?"

"Yeah?"

"The message he was given just before his big race really hit home for me." I took a deep breath. "The note read, 'It says in the old Book, He that honors me, I will honor.' "

"But, couldn't you show Zion just once?"

"Lorraine, whatever honor Zion might win at Nationals is less important to me than God's honor."

A couple days later, the new issue of a bimonthly magazine about giant schnauzers arrived. In that *Giant Steps* was a full-page article and picture of Zion and me. In large, block letters the title proclaimed, "Zion: Only on Sunday."

The article read, "Zion's owner/handler Joy Matthews is a Seventh Day Adventist, so they do not show Zion on Saturday. Often Zion goes to church with Joy and helps in the children's classroom demonstrating obedience and spiritual lessons from different commands. His favorite thing is going to each child and letting them pet him." It went on to tell about Zion's winnings.

ZION

only on Sunday

Zion's owner handler Joy Matthews is a Seventh Day Adventist so they do not show Zion on Saturday. Often Zion goes to church with Joy & helps in the children's classroom demonstrating obedience and spiritual lessons from different commands. His favorite thing is going to each child and letting them pet him.
Shown winning a Group 2 under Mr. Lowell Davis at Rogue Valley K.C. As of May 31st 1993 Zion has 19 B.O.B., one Group 2. One Group 4 & B.O.B. over B.I.S. Special onto a Group 3 at Inland Empire K.C. He has been undefeated since November 1992.

Zion gets a full page in *Giant Steps,* a magazine about giant schnauzers. The magazine goes to an International audience.

Amazement filled me. People throughout the United States and Europe would be reading about Zion, about Sabbath. The article made me all the more determined to honor God's Sabbath, whatever the cost. And to witness for Christ whenever the opportunity arose.

Del and I and our gentle giantt arrived with our travel trailer at the site of Nationals on Friday afternoon. On Sabbath we'd go to church. Even though Zion would miss the Nationals competition, many of the dogs would stay around for the Regionals on Sunday and Monday.

After we got settled, I left Del and Zion in the trailer, took the show schedule, and walked past row after row of RVs. I went to the showring area to case out where I needed to be Sunday morning. Since it was an All Breeds show, dogs of all sizes and descriptions were in crates by the RVs, or looking out RV windows, or on leashes held by their owners or handlers.

That, of course, was understood. It wasn't just a rule that dogs on the show grounds must be on a leash or in a crate at all times. It was a safety precaution. A serious dog fight could tear the participating dogs to shreds.

I kept my eyes open for giant schnauzers. When I spotted the occasional giant, I looked it over. Even though we wouldn't show at Nationals, my hopes for a win at Regionals on Sunday grew.

It was hot and humid that Friday afternoon. After I figured out where we'd be showing, I strolled back.

As I approached our trailer, I saw the door standing open. I assumed Del must be holding it while he looked out at something. As I got closer, I saw that Del was not in the doorway. Somehow the door had opened. My heart skipped a beat.

Where's Zion?

Then I saw him. By himself. Bounding away from the trailer like the curious, full-of-energy, little-more-than-a-pup that he was.

I glanced left. Nothing out of the ordinary that direction. Glanced right. Two huge rottweilers were straining at their leashes as they pulled a petite owner toward Zion.

Winner?

"ZION!" I CALLED, trying to keep the terror out of my voice. Visions of a terrible dogfight exploded in my mind.

Zion turned his head and looked my way.

"Come!"

Practically before the word was out of my mouth, Zion wheeled and headed at a run straight toward me.

I held the door. Zion zipped past me into the trailer. As I stepped inside and pulled the door closed behind me, the rottweilers rounded the end of our trailer.

Del looked up from a magazine, shock on his face.

"Go-o-d!" I praised Zion. "That was go-o-d!" I praised him, petted him, and gave him a handful of treats.

"How'd Zion get out?" I asked Del.

"I don't know. I didn't know he was out till he came bounding in."

"Maybe the door wasn't quite latched," I said. Zion often lay by the door. "Maybe he leaned against it and it opened so he went exploring."

"Maybe," Del responded.

"Whatever . . ." I looked upward. "Thank You, God. Thank You! Thank You for Carla's advice in Zion's first training class. Thank You that we kept practicing 'Come.' That he responded instantly. Thank You for protecting him!"

"Amen," Del added.

I told Del about the other dogs. "When I called Zion," I finished, "he was so intent on obeying me that he never even saw the other dogs."

"Praise God for that!" Del said.

In the midst of my thanksgiving a new thought hit. I sighed. "I may not know why God asks a thing of me. But I need to be so in tune with Him that it's first nature to obey Him instantly. My not seeing danger doesn't mean there isn't any."

Del nodded. "Good point," he said thoughtfully.

The next morning mixed feelings fought within me. I heard the sounds of a dog show camp: dogs barking (from tiny yips to barrel-chested bellows), blow-dryers blowing, people talking, motor home generators running, the hustle and bustle of people getting their dogs ready for the ring. This time the sounds were magnified because of the size of the group gathered for Nationals.

Del and I took Zion to church. Zion and I told the children's story. I'd been getting complaints from adults in churches in which I told children's stories. "Some of us older folk would like to pet him too," they'd said. So at the end of the story I asked the children, "How many of you would like to pet Zion?" Hands burst upward.

"Zion loves to have you pet him," I said. "Right after church, Zion and I will be just outside the front door on the lawn. Anybody who wants to pet him can meet us there."

After church Del answered questions, and children mobbed Zion. He looked one child in the eye, then another, and wagged his stub tail. Teenagers to oldsters swarmed around and joined the petting. *If kids and animals go together,* I thought, *it looks like a kid can come in any age.* By the time the last question was answered, the parking lot was nearly empty.

As we started toward our van, I noticed a white-haired, fragile-looking woman in a wheelchair. Her head was bent for-

If kids and animals go together, **I thought,** *looks like a kid can come in any age.*

ward so far I couldn't see her eyes. Remembering the delight of the man we'd visited in the nursing home, I turned toward her. As Zion and I neared, I asked the lady pushing her wheelchair, "Might your friend like to pet Zion?"

"She won't be able to pet him," the caregiver replied. "She's 103 years old, and she can't move her hands. But she always liked animals. I'll bet she'd like to see him."

I knelt in front of the wheelchair. "Would you like to see my dog?"

The woman's head raised slightly. A smile played at the edges of her lips.

Suddenly Zion took things into his own paws. He stepped forward, laid his chin gently in the woman's lap, and rolled his eyes up. Her arm moved slightly. I helped her lay her hand on Zion's soft head. She looked into his face and moved her hand slightly, petting Zion as best she could. The soft lines in her face turned into a vibrant smile.

Deep satisfaction flooded through me. I couldn't get her smile out of my mind all afternoon. I marveled at Zion. *How did he know exactly what that woman needed?*

Most giants were either macho or gentle—not both. Zion was alert and macho in the showring. But when someone petted him, especially a child or an elderly person, he melted. That had to be a God thing.

Sunday morning when Zion and I neared the ring where giant schnauzers would be shown shortly, heads started turning. With handlers and dogs from across the nation, there were a lot of both I'd never seen. Handlers unfamiliar to me stared at Zion.

"I don't remember seeing your dog yesterday," one handler said as we waited.

"No," I said, "we were in church yesterday. He helped me tell a story for children."

His brows knit into a question mark. "But why didn't you show him at Nationals?"

"I believe Saturday is God's Sabbath," I said. "We never show on Sabbath."

"Well, uh, I'm not into religious stuff," he said. "But I can't believe . . ." His voice trailed off as he shook his head.

"By the way," I puzzled, "there were more than 100 giant schnauzers registered for yesterday's show. How did you know this one wasn't here?"

"He has a-a presence about him." The man struggled for

words. "Don't know how to describe it. He moves so well. He's a beautiful dog, and he just walked in here like he knew he was the top dog. Sort of a kingly bearing. I *knew* I hadn't seen that yesterday."

While we talked, other handlers stared as if wondering, *Where in the world did this dog come from?*

I looked around at the other dogs waiting. *Zion could be headed for a big win.*

Then it was showtime. We took our places. We ran our paces as a group and individually. The judge, whom I didn't know, opened each dog's mouth and examined its teeth. He felt the dog for structure. We ran the circle again.

The judge finally called, "Winner." He pointed to an improperly groomed giant with poor movement and topline. I'd noticed him outside the ring and wondered why his owners even bothered to show him.

I stood there stunned.

All the other handlers and dogs were leaving the ring. Zion and I fell into line.

I don't mind Zion's losing to a dog as good as he is. But to that? Matter of fact, most of the dogs in the ring were conspicuously better than the "winner."

CHAPTER 12

Victory

ZION MAY NOT HAVE WON anything, but he attracted all kinds of attention. I hadn't been out of the ring five minutes before two breeders asked about using him for stud service. A passel of questions hit Del and me.

One common line of questioning was, "Are you his owner?"

"Yes."

"Why haven't we seen him before?"

"We can't afford to travel the country. So far I've only shown him in the Northwest."

"How old is he?"

"He's 2 years and a month."

"Barely more than a pup. And look at him!" They looked Zion over from head to tail. "What line is he from?"

I was so happy about his breeding that I proudly recommended Charles and Lorraine's kennel.

"What did you say his name is?"

"Zion."

"That sounds familiar. Where could I have heard his name?"

"His picture and an article were in the last issue of *Giant Steps*."

"Oh, yes. I remember. But that picture didn't do him justice. He's astounding!"

A half hour after the show, we'd barely moved from ringside.

One man waited graciously till Zion's admirers moved on. "Ma'am," he started. "May I take a look at your dog too?"

"Sure."

He knelt by Zion, noting his coat, feeling his structure. He seemed quite familiar with the breed. When he stood he said, "I've been hearing a lot about this dog. Wanted to check him out for myself." He swallowed. "Have you ever considered selling him?"

I smiled. "Yes, sir, I have. And I've decided not to. You see, he's God's dog. He's not mine to sell."

I couldn't read the man's expression. He was quiet for a long moment. Then he reached for his back pocket. He pulled out his checkbook and opened it. He pulled a pen from his shirt pocket, signed a check, and tore it out. He held the check out for me to take. "All you've got to do is fill in the amount," he said. "Any amount."

My heart felt like it stopped, then jumped to my temples. My throat felt dry. "Thank you, sir," I said. "But, truly, he's not for sale."

He drew the check back and handed me a business card. "If you should ever change your mind, let me know."

When Del, Zion, and I finally headed toward our trailer, we overheard part of a conversation: "He's just a very political judge."

I looked to see who was talking—a well-known full-time handler who showed dogs all over the nation. "Don't worry about losing when he's the judge," the handler continued. "Those of us who know him knew who he'd pick before we ever showed up. But that show's done, and we can move on."

"Oh, great!" the other sneered. "Are we in for more of the same tomorrow?"

"No!" the first handler exclaimed. "Tomorrow's judge is honest. And he really knows giants. Whoever wins tomorrow will be a true champion."

Thank You, God, I prayed in my mind, *for letting me overhear that conversation!* When I was tempted to think grumbling thoughts about the morning's show, I reminded myself of the handler's remarks.

Some of the dogs left on Sunday, but 86 giant schnauzers still competed in Monday's show, including the one who had won Nationals on Saturday.

As I watched how the judge examined the giants and what dogs he eliminated first, I had to agree with the handler I'd overheard the day before. The finalists he chose in each show, truly appeared to be the best dogs.

When Zion and I were in the ring, my full attention was on him. All the dogs and handlers ran the circle; then we individually ran our dogs across the ring while the judge concentrated on that dog's movement. The judge examined each dog almost like he was giving it a physical. Then we ran the circle again.

Of our group of 10 giants, eight dogs were eliminated. Zion and one other got to go into the finals. I sucked in my breath. My heart did a happy little dance.

After two more groups, Zion and I were back in the ring for the finals. Twelve dogs and handlers ran their laps. The judge reexamined each dog. In the end, the judge announced, "Best of Breed," and pointed to Zion.

My heart stood still. Zion had just won Best of Breed over 85 other giant schnauzers, including the giant who'd won Best of Breed at Nationals on Sabbath.

That earned Zion the right to compete against the other Best of Breed dogs in the working group. Each was beautiful in its own right. If Zion won nothing, it was still a great honor just to have won the right to enter that competition.

We'd have a couple hours before the working group competition. Del went to lunch with Charles and Lorraine. Zion and I headed to the trailer. I lay down, rested a few minutes, then grabbed the latest issue of *Giant Steps.* I scanned a couple articles, then came to the list of the top 10 giants in the nation. Might I recognize any of the names from the current competitions?

I didn't at first. It was understandable. I kept up with the goings-on as much as I could, but my focus had to be on Zion—feeding, watering, pottying, grooming, keeping him cool, keeping him relaxed, keeping him focused. I had to keep the treats in my pocket supplied, choose the right arm band for the right competition, and make sure Zion and I were doing the right thing at the right place at the right time.

At number 7 on the list, I did a double take.

Zion. The top 10 was beyond my biggest dream. Without showing on Sabbath, Zion had made the top 10. My head whirled.

"Oh, God, I can hardly fathom this. I show him so little. How can it be?"

Seek ye first, He responded.

"And all these things shall be added unto you," I whispered. "But the top 10?"

It's such fun giving gifts that are exceedingly abundantly more than a person's wildest imagination.

I could feel God's smile.

I didn't get much of a nap. I just lay there feeling overwhelmed . . . and grateful . . . and in shock.

We made it to group competition in plenty of time and waited outside the ring. Finally Del, Charles, and Lorraine showed up.

Looking at Charles and Lorraine, I asked, "Have you seen this year's top 10?"

"No," they both said. Lorraine added, "Is this year's out?"

"Yes. And Zion's on the list!"

"Zion?" they chorused.

"Yes."

"But how?" Lorraine asked. "You don't show him that much."

"That was my reaction," I said.

Del asked, "Top 10?"

"He's among the top 10 scoring giantt schnauzers in the nation," Lorraine explained.

"Zion?" Del asked. "The top 10 in the nation?"

"Yes," Lorraine answered. "That's a list every breeder wishes their dogs would hit! What an honor!"

Just then the attendant called, "Working group."

More points than any other giant schnauzer . . . even without competing in Nationals.

Zion and I headed for our places. After the paces and the examinations, the judge pointed at Zion. "Group 1," he announced.

Zion had just won first place. He'd earned more points than any other giant schnauzer during the entire weekend, including the Nationals competition on Sabbath.

Zion attracted a lot of attention again. Del eventually took off to wander around a few more booths. I headed for our trailer and sat down in a lawn chair to rest my legs and to really grasp what had just happened. I petted Zion and gave him the half-dozen treats I still had in my pocket.

"My ugly duckling puppy!" I said, patting his neck. "I just wanted to share you at Vacation Bible Schools." Zion looked up at me. I scratched him under his chin, just back of his beard where he especially liked to be scratched. "And even when I started showing you, everybody said you'd never get very far if I didn't show you on Saturdays." Zion's stub tail wiggled back and forth. "But look what God did!"

I leaned back in the chair and closed my eyes.

Del showed up before long. He handed me a half dozen advertising flyers and a couple magazines. "Here's a few more things I picked up at the booths."

Del started to put things away, to get ready for the trip home. Feeling too exhausted to get up, I flipped through one of the magazines. Then I started thumbing through the other. A headline caught my attention:

"Pedigree Awards
January-May"

I glanced down.

"Top Male of Pedigree Award
Zion, giant schnauzer
Owner: Joy Matthews"

"Del," I squealed, sitting up straight. "Look at this!"

He finished folding a chair, leaned it against the back of the trailer, and joined me.

I held the page up to him, pointing. "See?"

"Top Male of Pedigree Award," he read. "Wow!" he said with a grin. "I thought he'd won about enough for one day! What's this award?"

"It's points," I said. "Combined points. That means from January to May he got more points than any other male giant schnauzer across the nation."

"But, how could he? You don't show him that much."

I started counting on my fingers. "I showed Zion only 13 times in those five months."

"How many shows were there?"

I thought back. "Most of his competitors were probably in 25 or more." I looked down at Zion, lying contented beside me. With wonder, I added, "In half as many shows, he still won more points than any other of the best dogs out there."

Part of a Bible text popped into mind. Something about God's being "able to do exceeding abundantly above all that we ask or think" (Ephesians 3:20, KJV). "It's gotta be a God thing!" I said. "This is surely exceedingly abundantly more than anything I ever asked or thought!"

I finally got up to help ready the trailer for travel. A few minutes later, Charles and Lorraine showed up. "Joy," Lorraine started.

She was as serious as I'd ever seen.

"You've done a marvelous job with Zion! We just want you to know that we won't pressure you anymore to show him on your Sabbath."

I caught my breath.

"We will support you," she continued, "no matter what you do with him."

A weight lifted off my heart. This victory felt bigger and better than any award or blue ribbon.

We visited. After a bit, Lorraine hollered toward the driving lane between rows of trailers, "Dianne!"

A woman walking by turned. "Hey, Lorraine. Charles." She walked over. The three chatted briefly before Lorraine asked, "Have you met Joy and Zion?"

She smiled at me, then glanced down at Zion. "Oh, he's the one that just won Best of Breed."

"Right," Lorraine said.

"Fine-looking dog! I was impressed!" She knelt and took a good look at Zion.

Lorraine turned toward me. "Dianne's from Georgia. She has giants, too."

Discussion flowed easily—the top giant schnauzer winners here and at recent shows, grooming techniques, judges.

Dianne stopped midsentence and looked straight at me. "Can you come to Nationals in Georgia next year?"

"I don't know. When is it?"

She gave me a date. "Nationals is on Saturday, Regionals on Sunday and Monday—just like here."

Lorraine spoke up before I got my mouth open. "She won't be there on Saturday for Nationals. That's her Sabbath." She turned my way. "But you could go for the Sunday and Monday shows again."

"Perhaps," I said.

Dianne spoke again. "I'd love to have you come." Her smile disappeared. Her eyes wandered for a moment with a faroff look, then came back to meet mine again. She winked. "I'm chair of the committee that hires judges next year."

The next few weeks, every time I saw Dianne's business card or even thought about our conversation, it bugged me. *This is politics!* one corner of my mind shouted. *You didn't go out seeking it,* another voice soothed.

A couple months later Zion and I were in the ring for another competition. The dog just ahead of us was a poor excuse for a giant. Previously Zion had easily won over him. *At least he's no competition,* I thought. Then I remembered one of his other problems. *Give him space,* I told myself. *He was terribly slow last time.*

When the dogs started running the circle, I waited till the dog ahead and his handler were nearly halfway around before Zion and I started. Narrowing the gap fairly rapidly, Zion and I slowed. When Zion was about three giant schnauzer lengths behind, the other dog whirled around, jerking his handler off balance. A guttural growl sent chills up my spine. The dog's eyes were fire. He lunged toward Zion's neck.

Grumbling

ZION PLANTED HIS FEET. He glared at the dog flying toward him.

Help, Lord! my mind screamed.

The handler regained his balance. He braced himself, then jerked on the snarling dog's leash.

A soft but deep announcement rumbled from Zion's throat—the warning of a committed guard dog who's not looking for a fight but will face it if an attacker insists.

I held Zion's leash taut. It would be an ugly scene if the two dogs tangled. Zion had never fought anything. He was kind, gentle. But giant schnauzers are big—each of these was about 100 pounds. They are muscular, strong. As guard dogs, a good giant will not back down . . . even if its life is in danger.

Lord, help!

Three inches from Zion's nose the other dog's leash jerked him to a stop. The handler struggled to hold him.

The judge turned and pointed toward the attacking dog. "Winner," she announced.

Winner? my mind screamed as I left the ring. *He should have been dismissed!*

"What was the judge thinking?" I asked a handler who'd seen the whole thing from the sidelines.

"Thinking?" he sneered. "She wasn't."

"It sure didn't seem like it," I said. "To begin with, the dog was a loser."

"She's very political." The handler shrugged his shoulders. "It doesn't matter what the dog looks like for that judge, if there's a dog in the ring from that kennel, it'll win no matter what it does or how bad it looks."

I shook my head. "Why do they hire a judge like that?"

"Wel-l-l," The handler sighed. He took a deep breath. "Money . . . and clout?"

"Sounds like 'buying' a championship."

"Some championships are won fair and square and some aren't," he added. "Your dog, for instance. The fact that you're not spending a lot of money on him and he's still winning, says a great deal about how good a dog he really is."

I didn't usually spend much time with anger, but this time, I was mad. All afternoon I fumed every time I thought about it, and I could hardly get the politicking off my mind.

I replayed the scene in my mind. *What could I have done differently?*

Late that afternoon I spotted Paul. I told him about the current conundrum. "What could I do in the future?" I asked.

"Three things," he said. "Watch. Watch. Watch." He shook his head. "Knowing that dog and knowing that handler, I don't think the handler set out to do you dirt. I'd just about bet he didn't know that dog. Those of us who know him won't show him—for any price." His eyes narrowed. "I'm sorry about this situation, Joy, but the setup last year at this same show still makes me want to spit nails."

"Last year?"

"The two handlers that caught you in the middle, trying to set Zion up to make him hate other dogs."

"You think that's what they were doing?"

"Yes, I do."

H'mmm. Several situations replayed in my mind. "Early on," I said, "no other dogs ever bothered Zion or me. But lately, between shows, big dogs have bumped into him frequently. Occasionally a handler says, 'Excuse me.' But, usually, they act as if they didn't notice. Could they too be trying to set him up?"

Paul sighed deeply. "Could well be."

"In fact," I added, "just this morning a bullmastiff bumped Zion in the rear. And Zion turned and growled."

"That may be exactly what they're trying to do," he said. "Zion is an unusual dog. He's honest best in show material. There's not another giant out there who can honestly beat him."

I sucked in my breath. Paul—an honest handler who truly loved good dogs—had no reason to say Zion was the best dog if he didn't believe it.

Paul continued. "But every time Zion wins, they don't. If they can get him to growl at other dogs, he may growl in the ring, and judges may think he's vicious. If Zion gets thrown out, they'll quit losing to him."

"Are you telling me that some of the handlers would ruin a great dog because of their own greed?"

Paul looked off into the distance like he was weighing his words. "There are a lot of great handlers and judges who make dog showing a real honor. But yes, there are some rotten eggs, too."

I sighed. "What could I have done to avoid the problem?" I asked.

"Had a working set of eyes in the back of your head." He shook his head. "Watch the dog behind as best you can. If one's getting too close, ask the handler to back off. If the dog keeps coming, step in between the two dogs."

"What would the judge think about my getting out of line?"

"If it's a worthwhile judge, they'll understand you're saving your dog. If not, well, your dog's worth protecting, no matter what the judge thinks."

"Good point," I said, nodding. "Zion's worth it!"

"He definitely is!"

Paul's realistic words helped cool my fuming. Some of the owners and handlers were kind, friendly, and helpful. They had been an important part of Zion's success. Paul's advice was timely.

After the attack, Zion seemed to think that other large dogs in a showring were out to get him. As a guard dog, he wasn't about to be pushed around without voicing his opinion. His grumble was not quite a growl, but close enough that handlers began complaining, "Can't you keep your dog quiet?" And when judges opened the mouth of this 95 pounds of muscle to examine his teeth and he looked them in the eye and grumbled, some got a little wary. Especially after another giant schnauzer attacked a judge one day.

"He's vicious!" some handlers accused.

Even though I knew it wasn't true, it hurt to have people think it. Or did they believe it? The truth was so obvious. Zion would stand up to another giant in the ring, then, six feet from the gate, he'd melt into some child's hug. And if they could only see Zion at home—if Del's three-and-a-half pound toy Chihuahua had decided to sleep in Zion's bed, Zion would lie down on the floor rather than bother him.

I tried everything I could think of to quiet Zion in the ring. He still grumbled. I called Lorraine. We discussed the problem, and she suggested a trainer that might have some ideas.

We were about to hang up when Lorraine asked, "Joy, what do you do when your world falls apart?"

"What's going on, Lorraine?"

"My daughter made a choice that could ruin her life," she said. She described the problem. "What can I do?"

We visited. I did my best to encourage Lorraine, and assured her I would pray. By the end of the conversation both Lorraine and I were more positive.

But nothing I did stopped Zion's grumbling. Eventually some other giant schnauzer owners recommended a trainer in an-

Bosom buddies—Zion and Tazz.

other state. "She stopped my rottweiler from growling," one said. "She was good and fair with my dog. I highly recommend her." In desperation I made arrangements and drove Zion there "In a month," she assured me, "we'll have his growling stopped."

When I went to get Zion, the trainer showed me the methods she'd been using. One was to set Zion up in a situation where he'd grumble. When he did, she'd do something to surprise him—such as throw a chain over his head.

Though the chain thrown over his head didn't actually hurt Zion, I was appalled.

"You've *got* to keep doing this!" she insisted. "Set him up for a situation where he'll grumble, then throw the chain over his head. Do it every day. He has to know that something awful will happen every time he does it. If not, he'll go right back to grumbling."

Three problems: First, he still grumbled. Second, I couldn't throw a chain over his head in the showring and that was the main place he grumbled; and third, I despised the idea of setting him up to fail and then doing something awful to him.

"Call me," the trainer said, "to let me know how your daily practice is going." She probably sensed my hesitation. "This is the *only* way," she emphasized again, "that you'll be able to keep showing him!"

My heart was heavy as I drove Zion home. I'd raised him with love and kindness. I'd never have taken him to that trainer if I'd realized how she would treat him. I felt like I'd betrayed my gentle giant.

When we get home, I wondered, *what should I do?*

Wait

ZION SNOOPED AROUND THE HOUSE and romped around the fenced yard like it was great to be home. The first time I tried a setup with him and tossed the chain over his head, he looked shocked. Even though it tore at my heart, we practiced daily.

At the next show, Zion growled. I telephoned the trainer again. "Keep practicing," she advised. "It's your only hope."

One morning I agonized with God. "What should I do God?"

Wait, I heard the Lord whisper.

"Wait?" I questioned. In my prayer journal I wrote, "Wait. Carla taught 'Wait' in the class Zion and I went to when he was just a pup. 'One of your jobs as a dog's master,' Carla said, 'is to protect your dog. The command "Wait" is very important. Before you get out of a vehicle, before you go around a corner, before you go out a door, have your dog "Wait." You go ahead. When you are sure it's safe for your dog, then you can release it.' "

Zion and I had practiced the "Wait" command. I agreed it was valuable. "But God," I asked, "what are you trying to tell me now?"

Wait before Me, He answered.

"Wait before You?"

I waited in the silence. Suddenly I burst out, "Wait! When

I wait before You in the morning in the Bible and in prayer, You're checking out what my day will bring. The reason You ask me to wait before You is that You can protect me. You want to direct me to avoid dangers. Right?"

That's an important part of it.

"And that's another story idea!" I exulted. "Wait before the Lord. And Zion already knows how to demonstrate it!"

Later that day I practiced "Wait" with Zion. He stood tall, his ears up, his eyes focused on the treat I tossed on the grass three feet in front of him. But he waited. The instant I said, "Get it," he bounced to the treat and devoured it. Practicing "Wait" was fun.

Zion and I played ball. He raced after the ball, often caught it midair, then raced back to me for more fun and games. We both loved our times together.

Then came the time I dreaded. I set him up. As soon as he grumbled, I threw the chain over his head. Instantly Zion stopped grumbling. He wheeled around. Looking directly into my eyes, he growled.

My heart sank. "Oh, God," I cried, "what have I done? He's Your dog. Have I ruined him?"

The next day Zion and I were scheduled to tell another children's story. *Will he even do what I ask?* I wondered.

Usually Zion followed me around. If I was in the living room, he was too. If I went to the kitchen, he tagged along and lay down nearby. But that evening, he lay in the family room, paying little attention to where I was or what I was doing. My heart ached.

"God," I pleaded, "please forgive me. Please help me know what to do with Your dog. If I'm supposed to stop showing him, that's fine with me. But please help him not to be ruined for doing Your work."

Sabbath morning when I got out Zion's storytelling scarf, he bounced toward me, his tail wagging.

I knelt down. "Have you forgiven me, Zion?"

He moved closer and leaned his head into my neck. I threw my arms around him and wept.

Later at church the kids loved the story. Zion acted his part like a pro. I thanked God over and over.

The next morning, Zion and I went to the show we had registered for. In the ring, as we waited for action, I heard God whisper *Wait.*

I looked at Zion. He was glancing at the other dogs.

"Zion," I said.

His eyes snapped toward me.

"Wait." I tossed a treat a couple feet in front of him.

Zion's eyes went to the treat. He stood tall and still, his ears alert.

"Go-o-d," I encouraged. "Go-o-d."

Zion stood tall and still, his eyes focused, his ears up. He wasn't saying a word.

"Get it," I said after a minute.

He bolted ahead and wolfed down the treat.

"Zion," I said, before he had time to get his attention back on his surroundings. "Wait." We repeated the exercise until the judge started the run around the ring.

Zion was a perfect gentleman that day. He earned his fortieth Best of Breed.

At home I telephoned the trainer again to report on Zion's grumbling. I told her what I'd done at the show. How quiet and alert Zion was.

"So," I asked, "what should I do now?"

The phone line was quiet. "Well," she finally responded, "I guess do what works."

"Thank You, God!" I squealed as I clicked the phone off.

Zion looked up at me.

I leaned over and held his head in both hands. "The chain is history!"

Every time I thought about the upcoming Nationals, World War III erupted in my mind. *There's politics! . . . I didn't seek it . . . But is the organizer trying to influence a judge on Zion's behalf? I didn't do anything wrong . . . Neither did I make my stance clear.*

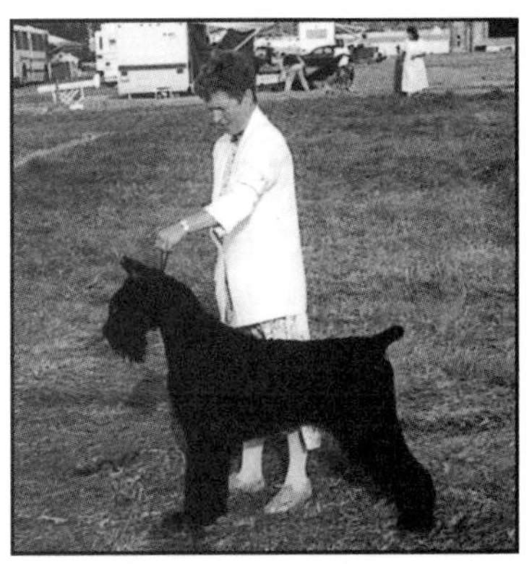

"Zion, Wait." After the initial success, we practiced between shows near the camp of dog owners and handlers.

Occasionally I asked God what I should do. But I didn't listen very long for an answer.

Even though we'd miss the Nationals competition on Sabbath, I felt certain that Zion would come home with another big win from the Sunday or Monday show. I registered him for those.

Thinking about the Nationals reminded me of the last one. While Nationals competition was going on, Zion helped tell a children's story, greeted a bundle of young and not-so-young, and gave a 103-year-old woman's tired face the glow of sunshine. That reminded me of the joy of the man we'd visited in a nursing home one Sabbath afternoon in Boise. "Thank you, lady, for bringing your dog! This is the best day I've had in a good long time!"

When a local nursing home Activities Director telephoned, Zion and I started visiting on the first Wednesday afternoon of each month.

Zion seemed to sense what the different individuals needed. Week after week his visits left a wake of smiles and brightened eyes. I was tempted sometimes to call and say I couldn't make it, but I sensed that going was important. That cheering the elderly was, somehow, a gift we could give to God. So we went, come snow or 100-degree temperatures.

Before I let people approach, I was always careful to ask them if they wanted to pet Zion. Almost always. One Wednesday afternoon Zion marched into a room I hadn't planned to visit. He walked right up to the wheelchair-bound resident and laid his head in her lap. Her vacant stare didn't change. Zion didn't move. After several minutes the woman looked down at him. He still didn't move. Several more minutes passed before she lifted her hand to Zion's head and began petting him. His tail wagged. The woman's dull eyes brightened. Zion soaked up her petting and stayed right there for more. After a long time the woman started talking to Zion.

At one point I heard steps at the door, then a gasp. As I turned, a nurse fled.

What dreadful thing have we done? I wondered. I looked around the room. Nothing was noticeably wrong. I glanced at the door. No signs indicated we should have stayed out. I felt like we should go, yet there was something almost reverent about the conversation this woman was having with Zion.

I was still trying to figure out how to exit gracefully when a nursing assistant came to wheel the woman to dinner. As Zion and I headed down the hall, I heard steps behind us.

"Ma'am," the nurse said when she caught up with us, "you may not know what you just did, but that woman hadn't spoken a word to anyone in five months! We've tried everything. You and your dog just did the impossible!"

Month by month, bringing joy to others brought joy to me.

A few weeks before the Georgia Regionals I called Dianne, knowing that different judges like different things. "What's the judge on Sunday like? How should I groom Zion?"

"It doesn't make any difference," Dianne said. "That judge likes me."

Alarms went off in my mind. Again. I tried to ignore them.

The Sabbath of Nationals, Zion and I told a children's story.

As usual after Zion and I told a story, children mobbed him. He looked one child in the eye, and then another. He thrived on their attention.

Sunday, with great expectations, I showed Zion. He won nothing. *Oh, well, there's another day.*

That afternoon I picked up the magazine with the top 10 listing. Even though I'd only shown Zion 31 times that year, I was curious. I stood there and thumbed through the magazine till I found the list. Zion was number 4!

Surely he'll win tomorrow, I thought. *He is, after all, the number 4 dog in the nation.*

Monday morning Zion and I arrived at the show grounds early. I left nothing to chance. I groomed him to perfection. In the heat and humidity I worked hard to keep him cool. No dog in the ring was better than him. But Zion didn't win.

I was so sure he would win. *He's a great dog!* I thought. *And what did Dianne mean?*

"Why, Lord?" I questioned. And I was desperate enough to listen.

What I heard was another question: *Would you have wanted him to have a questionable win on his record?*

Yes!

"WOULD I HAVE WANTED ZION to have a questionable win on his record?" I asked aloud.

The breath stuck in my throat. My head whirled. The magnitude of my decision not to worry about politics when Zion would benefit, hit me hard.

Then relief washed over me. There'd been losses when Zion didn't deserve to lose. But every win was fair and square. "Thank You, God, for protecting us!"

Memories of other dogs winning unfairly flooded over me. Anger welled up in my chest.

But, Joy, God said with a gentle voice, *is it possible that some of the political handlers and judges started out with something that seemed small? Might others have gotten caught up in politics just one little step at a time?*

"Just like me," I whispered. I closed my eyes. My breaths came slow and shallow. "God, forgive me. 'There, but for the grace of God, go I.' Forgive me for letting ribbons and awards become more important than Your way of doing things."

I sensed Gods arm around my shoulder.

Gladly.

"Forgive me for not seeking You first."

Done.

My heart ached. The silence seemed deafening. An occasional tear slipped down one cheek or the other. Finally I cried out again, "O, God, forgive me!"

I already did!

Tears flowed. God hadn't held back His mercy because of my selfishness. He poured His forgiveness freely over every bit of my selfishness.

A bigger sense of God's love filled me. A feeling of cleanness washed over me. I basked in peace. Then I questioned, "God, how am I supposed to think about the handlers whose dogs bumped Zion purposely?"

Ideas began to form in my mind. I can't do anything to change others. They're God's responsibility, not mine. "So what's my responsibility?" I asked.

Seek ye first . . .

"My responsibility," I said aloud, "is to seek first the kingdom of God and His righteousness. To act like Jesus, no matter what others do. To let God be responsible for His other kids."

"My responsibility," I continued, "is never, never, never to be involved in the politics of dog showing in any way ever again."

It felt like heavy weights dropped off my shoulders. As if I could spread my arms wide and run free in the sunshine for miles.

"But how should I think about those who have wronged Zion and me?" I asked.

I realized how quickly God responded to me with forgiveness. Jesus had already made it possible. The instant I acknowledged my need for forgiveness, it was done.

"Forgiveness was already available before I recognized my need," I whispered. "God, would You please put that kind of forgiveness in my heart for those who have hurt Zion and me?"

At that moment I truly wanted to forgive. *But what will happen when I'm at a show and I see one of those handlers? Or worse, when some handler gets his dog to bump Zion?*

"You'll have to put Your forgiveness in my heart then, too!" I said.

As for the Nationals, since they were always on Sabbath, there wasn't any point in flying all over the country to go to the other shows connected with them. Missing the pressure connected with the Nationals would feel like a blessing.

Besides, I had plenty to do. We'd acquired Zion's half-sister, Frolic, and had raised a litter of her pups. Two pups went to Charles and Lorraine, and we kept two—Summer and Kelah.

Both pups were well on their way to championships. Kelah was an especially gorgeous young dog. Before she was a year old, I'd had several serious offers to buy her.

Initially, I decided to keep Kelah. But she was a pesky pup—she constantly wanted attention. And if she didn't get it, she'd pull the cushions off the couch and chew them to bits . . . or pull down the legal documents I'd laid on the back of the couch for "just a minute" and mark them with her toothy signature.

As Kelah's winnings increased, her value as a show dog increased too. I'd already been offered $5,000.00.

"I'm ready to sell Kelah," I told Del over dinner one evening.

Del was surprised, but he had no argument with paying off our bills.

I telephoned Lorraine to let her know Kelah was available. Often when we talked I reminded Lorraine that I prayed regularly for her daughter. This time, when she recognized my voice, she bubbled, "I so much appreciate your praying for my daughter, Joy. She's making some better choices. She made it through a major crisis yesterday. I just hope shell keep making good decisions."

"We can keep praying," I said. "That'll help."

"Indeed," she responded. "I will. And I know you will, too."

At shows I watched for the breeders who'd earlier expressed interest in buying Kelah. I also expected to let others know about Kelah at an animal training seminar I attended. But I got so excited about the training, that I forgot everything else.

The teachers used the clicker method to train dolphins, whales, birds, and other creatures. The more I listened and observed, the more excited I got.

Many dog trainers in the past had used force. To get a dog to sit, they would physically push its hindquarters down. To get it to come, they would jerk on its leash. It didn't take the dog much thinking to realize that if the trainer or owner was across the yard, they couldn't force them. So the dog would do what it wanted to when no one was physically present beside them to force obedience. As a result, punishment became a major part of much training.

The clicker method, instead, used positive reinforcement. For instance, if you wanted a dolphin to jump over a bar, you put a bar on the bottom of the pool. When the dolphin accidentally swam over it, you clicked the clicker and threw a fish. (For a dolphin, the clicker was connected to an underwater and above-water speaker system so the click could be heard both in or out of the water.) Next time it swam over the bar, you clicked the clicker and threw a fish. Before long the dolphin figured out that every time it swam in that particular spot, it heard a specific sound. And every time it heard the sound, it got a fish.

Then the trainer raised the bar a bit. The same process continued. The trainer raised the bar further. Within a few training sessions the bar was high enough so the dolphin could swim under it, but the dolphin soon learned it got a click and a fish only when it swam over the bar.

When the dolphin understood the concept clearly, once in a while the click and fish were withheld. The dolphin learned that if it did the desired behavior, most of the time it would be rewarded. But if it didn't, there was no possibility of reward. This actually made obedience to a command more reliable.

Eventually the bar was high enough that the dolphin had to jump out of the water to go over it. But it was happy to do so because it got a click and a fish.

The dolphin learned a new behavior without any punishment, strictly by positive reinforcement.

As the trainers talked, in my mind I applied their practice and theories to dog training. And the more I heard, the more excited I got.

During one lunch break I met the director of the Pet Partnership Program at a women's prison in Washington state. Inmates there trained service dogs. Like me, she was excited about the potential.

"With clicker training," I exulted, "I can teach a dog to do *anything* it's physically capable of!"

"Yes!" she enthused, "and the dogs will be happy to do what they need to do! With a service dog it's especially important that the dog *want* to please its master."

I was excited about clicker training for the dog training I did for other people. But I was ecstatic as I thought about what I could teach Zion to do for audiences.

Like bow. When a dog gets up in the morning, the first thing it does is stretch. I could click and give Zion a treat. When he was doing it faithfully whenever I held the treat down for him, I could connect the command "Bow."

Like "Wave." Or "Give me five." On the way home my mind ran wild with things I could teach Zion.

Besides, many dog trainers had to quit their work when they were still quite young because their backs or arms would no longer handle the jerking and punishing they did with large dogs. When I got home I told Del, "I can train dogs until I'm 105!"

When Zion got up the next morning, I started clicking and rewarding his stretch. Within a few days, he had "Bow" down pat.

I tried to carry the clicker in my pocket all the time. But

Vavra Photography

"Zion, bow."

I soon discovered that sometimes I wanted to click and reward when the clicker was hard to get at. By the time I got my hands out of the dishwater and fished the clicker out of my pocket, Zion had gone on to something else, and I'd lost the opportunity to reward him for a behavior I wanted to encourage.

So what could I do? I always had my voice and it was never in bread dough or mop water.

I decided on a distinctive, quick, high-pitched, "Yes!" It would not be confused with a "yes" in conversation. And it would be appropriate and unobtrusive anyplace I could talk. Even in the middle of a children's story.

Clicker training, though I used a "Yes!" instead of a click, was the most exciting thing I'd learned about training. I bubbled over about it to most anyone who'd listen.

I told Joyce about the new training methods. At the end of the conversation, she changed the topic. "By the way, are you going to Nationals this year?"

"No," I responded without a second's hesitation.

"You should," she urged, "it's not on your Sabbath."

"It isn't?"

"No. It's on Wednesday."

I found a brochure about the Nationals. Indeed, they were on Wednesday—the first time ever. *Maybe I should go to support the decision to have them on a day other than Saturday,* I reasoned.

Soon I was back to "Yes!" training and sharing my new training method.

My friend Joanne was another person with whom I enjoyed dog talk. She had multiple sclerosis and was able to live in her own home because of her service dog. Her black Lab, Jubal, happily got the phone for her, held doors open, and picked up the myriad things she dropped because of her muscle deterioration.

One day when I exulted to Joanne on the phone about Zion learning to bow, she didn't express her usual enthusiasm. Then the problem came out: "Joy, I've got to retire Jubal."

Joanne and Jubal had been inseparable for eight years. Jubal's skill as a service dog was the reason she could live by herself in her own home.

"There's only one thing I don't like about Jubal," Joanne said. "He sheds so badly. There's dog hair all over the house. So when I get a new dog, I don't want another black Lab. Know what I've been thinking?"

"What?"

"I'd like a giant schnauzer."

We talked about what Joanne would need her dog to do—

things such as pick up the items Joanne dropped, help pull off her sweater or coat, get the phone and bring it to her.

"Do you think you could help me find one?" she asked.

"Sure," I said. "I'll make some calls."

We needed to find the new dog soon. Then it would need to go through specialized service dog training.

A lot of giant schnauzers didn't have the desire to serve and the loyalty that would be needed for doing the work of a service dog. Joanne's dog would need to come from a kennel where temperament was a major consideration in breeding.

I immediately started calling. I kept hearing "No, we don't have a dog that would work. But we'll keep you in mind."

At shows I talked to other owners. "We don't have any right now. We'll let you know if we hear of someone who does."

As the Nationals approached, I waffled back and forth with the decision of whether or not to go. "I want Your kingdom first," I told God. "Would this be for Your kingdom?"

I wanted to support the decision to have the Nationals on a day other than Saturday. *For Charles and Lorraine, if nothing else,* I finally decided. This time, though, the decision didn't grow out of obligation, but out of our deepening friendship.

As the Nationals got closer, I felt nervous—Zion still grumbled sometimes. Sometimes he didn't. The times he didn't were usually the times I was most on my toes with distracting him with "Wait." But not always.

The Wednesday morning of competition as I prepped Zion for his debut in a Nationals competition, my heart raced and my hands trembled. The responsibility of showing God's dog in the only Nationals he had been able to compete in, maybe the only Nationals he would *ever* get to show in, weighed heavily on me. I prayed as I worked. *Please keep him from growling. Please don't let other dogs get too close . . .*

CHAPTER 16

The Best Trophy

PLEASE DON'T LET ANY vicious dogs near him, I continued to pray as I readied Zion for the Nationals competition. *Please . . .*

Then I heard God's voice so clearly it almost seemed audible. *You are trying for an earthly trophy that will pass away,* He said. *The best trophy has already been won.*

Best trophy? I questioned.

I have a crown for you. I bought it with My blood.

I stopped fluffing the fur on Zion's legs, closed my eyes, and let the words settle in my mind.

That trophy will last forever.

Awe overpowered me. "And that's really the only trophy that matters," I whispered.

I can help Zion win all the trophies he needs. Just keep heaven the highest priority.

Tension drained out the soles of my feet. A peace I didn't fully understand replaced it. As I blow-dried, combed, fluffed, and sprayed Zion, I sang softly. "Seek ye first the kingdom of God and His righteousness . . ." I didn't know what awards might be added to Zion's list, but, frankly, it didn't matter.

I walked into the first competition feeling confident. Not confident that Zion would win. Confident that Zion was God's dog and that I was God's person and that the outcome was God's responsibility.

At the first competition Zion eyed another giant. "Zion," I said. He turned from the dog and looked at me. "Wait," I said. I tossed a treat a couple feet in front of him. He eyed it, but waited obediently for most of a minute. "Get it." He did. After another "Wait," it was time for competition.

I watched closely and did what I needed to do, but I enjoyed a freedom and peace I never before had experienced in the showring. When I had first started showing, I was nervous because I was inexperienced and was afraid I'd do something wrong. I was just starting to feel comfortable in the showring when Zion started "talking." Lately, I'd been a nervous wreck when showing. But that day, at the Nationals, when I normally would have been more nervous than ever before, I was totally at peace.

Zion made the first cut.

He got a lot of attention when we left the ring, and he loved every minute of it. Lots of people asked lots of questions. Many of the conversations went something like the one with another giant owner.

"What a gorgeous dog!" he exclaimed.

We talked a bit about giant schnauzers in general and Zion in particular. "But he's not just a beautiful show dog," I said. "We go to nursing homes and visit the elderly. And he goes with me to churches and helps me tell children's stories."

"To church?" he puzzled. "What would a dog do in church?"

"He demonstrates what I talk about," I said. "For instance, you know how important it is for a dog to come when called."

"Yes."

"How, in a dangerous situation, coming when called could save the dog's life."

"Yes."

"I tell children how important 'Come' is for a dog. Then I tell them that the most important thing they can do is to 'come' to Jesus."

A flicker of understanding lit in his eyes. "That's neat," he said.

Later, at the final competition, a female giant won Best of Breed. A flicker of disappointment crossed my mind. *It's OK,* I thought. *The best trophy has already been won.* A smile crept up from my heart. *Thank You, God.*

Then the judge called, "Best of Opposite." He turned and pointed to Zion. Zion had won Best Male Giant Schnauzer in the nation.

As Zion and I left, I carried the largest trophy Zion had won—a large silver bowl. But my heart carried a crown, a crown that would be there on the days Zion won *and* on the days he lost.

Minutes after we left the ring, Joyce caught up with Zion and me. "Good job!" she exulted. "A great win for anyone. Really prestigious for an owner who shows their own dog!"

A lot of the dogs stayed for the Regionals that followed the Nationals, on Thursday, Friday, Saturday, and Sunday. Three days in a row of shows was common. Four days in a row happened occasionally. Five was rare. We'd flown from Washington to Texas and planned to stay to the end. A service dog for Joanne was heavy on my mind—I planned to ask around for a giant schnauzer that would fill the bill.

Joanne was my friend. I loved her. With her disease, she had a specific need. To continue to live independently in her own home, she needed to replace her service dog. I wanted desperately to find the right dog for her.

To meet the qualifications, it had to be under two years old. It would have to be spayed or neutered, which meant it could not be shown. And to work as a service dog, it would need to want to please and to enjoy a one-on-one relationship with its owner.

I still kept hearing, "Sorry, but I don't have a dog now that would work for a service dog."

On Sabbath, Zion and I told a children's story in a local church. In the afternoon we visited a nursing home. As the sun set that evening, I realized I hadn't thought about dog shows all day.

Bringing happiness to someone else brought me more happiness than ribbons or trophies.

I used to look forward to Sabbaths ending so I could show Zion. But sharing Zion and the spiritual principles he illustrated was more satisfying than any ribbon or trophy he'd ever won. Bringing happiness to someone else brought me more happiness than any honor he'd ever earned.

At the Sunday show Zion was full of energy. He nearly pranced around the ring. Joyce and her giant were right behind us. "I can't believe my dog. He won't stand up straight. He won't hold his ears up right. He mopes around like he's all pooped out."

I couldn't help smiling to myself. *Yes, even dogs need Sabbath.*

We weren't far from the ring when Paul spotted us. He waved and headed our direction. "What a dog!" he enthused when we met. He reached down and petted Zion, then looked up. "Joy," he said. "I have a question for you."

"For me?" It had always been me asking *him* questions.

"Yeah," he said. "This one's for you." He paused an instant, then asked, "Why don't you ever show Zion on Saturday?"

I smiled. "Saturday is the Bible Sabbath," I said. "It's the day Jesus rested on. It's a special day for fellowship with Him."

Paul asked a lot of questions. And God gave me answers.

"Interesting," he said thoughtfully. "That really does make sense." He petted Zion again, then glanced at his wrist. "Uh-oh. I'd better get a move on. I've got an appointment in seven minutes." He started to turn, then turned back. "Thanks, Joy. I've been wondering about that."

"Good to talk to you, Paul."

I headed for home that evening. I knew I needed to call Joanne right away. She was expecting to hear about the various giants I'd found that she could choose from.

I put off calling her. A couple days after I got home, she called me. "I tried, Joanne. Honest. But I'm batting zero. I feel so . . ."

"Hey," she stopped me. "If you say you tried, of course, you tried. Relax. I'm not expecting you to manufacture a dog!"

She was upbeat. But she still needed a dog.

We were about to hang up when Joanne asked, "What about Kelah?"

"No," I responded instantly. "I'm going to sell her and pay off our bills." I paused. "Besides," I said, "I don't think she'd work."

Several times that afternoon my plans for Kelah cropped up in my thinking. Each time a discomfort badgered me.

The next morning in my quiet time, God led me to 1 John 3:17: "But whoever has this world's goods, and sees his brother in need, and shuts up his heart from him, how does the love of God abide in him?" (NKJV).

Joanne's need flashed into my mind. My breath caught. *It would be a major sacrifice to give up the income Kelah could provide. Surely God wouldn't ask that.*

I looked back to verse 16: "By this we know love, because He laid down His life for us" (NKJV).

I looked out the window. *God certainly knows the cost of* giant *gifts!*

I sighed deeply, then looked back to my Bible. "And we also ought to lay down our lives for the brethren" (NKJV).

I stared, unseeing, out the window; took a deep breath; and squirmed in my chair.

"My little children," the Bible continued, "let us not love in word or in tongue, but in deed and in truth" (verse 18, NKJV).

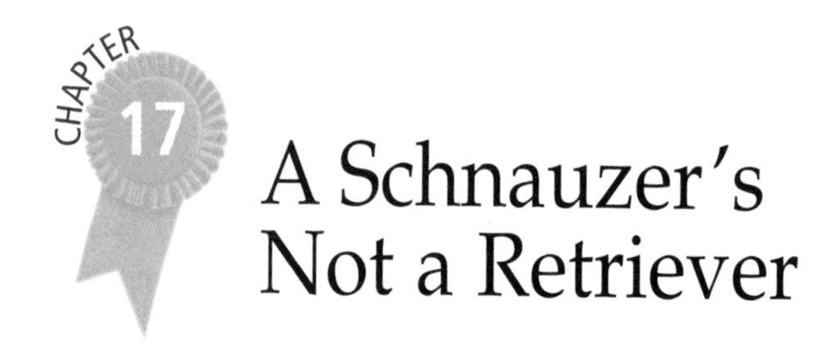

A Schnauzer's Not a Retriever

I DIDN'T EVEN BREATHE FOR A MOMENT.

If you have something someone else needs and won't give it to the person in need, God's love isn't in you.

The message drove deeper: I had a dog. My friend needed a service dog for her physical well-being.

"But Kelah's so pesky," I said. "Will she work for Joanne?"

I don't know the process God used, but as I took my next breath I knew in my innermost soul that God wanted me to give Kelah to Joanne . . . and *I* wanted to. I didn't know how Kelah would work, but I knew *who* I could trust.

"Thank You, God," I prayed, "for making it clear what I'm supposed to do. Thank You for providing this dog."

I dialed Joanne's phone number. I could hardly wait to tell her. *R-r-i-i-n-n-g-g.* Silence. *R-r-i-i-n-n-g-g.* Silence. *R-r-i-i-n-n-g-g.* Her answering machine came on. "This is Joy," I said. "Call me as soon as you get home!"

The morning plodded on. I called again. Answering machine. I went out into the yard to practice commands with Zion. He did fine. I couldn't keep *my* mind on whatever command he was supposed to be following or whatever game we played.

Inside, I checked our answering machine. Nothing. I tried Joanne's number again. Answering machine. I was bubbling over till I could hardly stand it. "Please, call me as *soon* as you can!" I urged. "Oh, yeah. This is Joy."

Eleven o'clock. The phone rang. I rushed to answer. "Hello?" I fairly shouted into the receiver.

The salesman seemed surprised by my initial enthusiasm.

I bounced off the wall most of the day. I kept the cordless phone in my pocket while I groomed a client's poodle. When I got home from a trip to town, I rushed to our answering machine. Joanne hadn't called. I could hardly stand the wait. I looked for the business card of the director of the Prison Pet Partnership Program, who I'd met at the clicker training seminar.

At 4:15 that afternoon, Joanne finally called. "What's going—"

"Joanne," I blurted when I heard her voice, "I want to give you Kelah!"

There was a pause. "You can't do that," she said.

"Yes, I can!" I exclaimed.

"But you need to pay off your bills."

"God will take care of us. I *want* to give her to you."

Joanne wasn't convinced easily. I finally shared the verses I'd read that morning. "I can't explain it, Joanne, but God gave me the desire to share Kelah. I *want* you to have her!"

Suddenly the explosion was on her end of the phone line. "Thank you, Joy! Oh, thank you! Are you sure you want to do this?"

There'd been no question in my mind before her call. But if I'd had an inkling of doubt, it would have been gone after hearing the joy in Joanne's voice. "Yes, Joanne. I'm positive!"

"Thank you! Thank you! That is so wonderful! Thank you, Joy! Oh, thank you!"

Ecstatic is much too calm a word for Joanne's mood!

The phone rang again about 6:30. "Thank you, Joy. I'm so excited! I can just hardly believe it! Thank you! Thank you so much!"

And at 9:00. "Thank you, Joy! I just had to tell you thank you one more time tonight!"

The next day, we started the ball rolling. The Prison Pet Partnership Program's director said, "Yes!" We worked out the details. Among other things, Joanne would need to send a letter telling them what she needed her service dog to be able to do.

I called the vet to get an appointment to have Kelah spayed. I swallowed hard in the middle of that conversation. Kelah was such a beautiful show dog. She was well on her way to championship. *But championship is nothing compared to serving,* I reminded myself. We set up the appointment.

At first Joanne called several times a day. "Thank you, Joy! I just had to thank you again!"

"You're welcome, Joanne. I'm so glad God helped me know that you and Kelah were right for each other."

"God's going to bless you for this, Joy."

"I've already gotten a blessing," I said. "The happiness in your voice was worth every penny Kelah could have brought!"

At the prison I got to deliver Kelah directly to the inmate who would train her as a service dog. Gail had trained other service dogs. I showed her the commands Kelah already knew. I watched Gail and Kelah interact. Gail was gentle yet in control, loving yet firm.

As I left for home I prayed, "Thank You, God, for working this out. Please help Kelah learn what she needs to know to help Joanne."

That spring a camp meeting teen leader called. "Would you and Zion do a feature every evening of camp meeting for our teen group?"

"Teens, did you say?"

Though my knees still knocked when I told a children's

story, God had given me the strength to make it through every time. I was beginning to believe that truly God could use me to help children understand spiritual principles. But teenagers? Did I have anything that teenagers would be interested in?

Every time I prayed for Gods wisdom on the matter, I felt more convinced that He was preparing the way I was to walk in. And that He would see me through. No matter how nervous I had ever been, God always blessed when I moved out in faith to share Jesus.

That spring Zion and I headed for dog shows again. Whenever Lorraine and I were at the same show, we looked each other up. One evening we relaxed in lawn chairs by her motor home. In the middle of a pleasant conversation, she groused about an acquaintance. "She may go along with you when you put some pressure on her," Lorraine said, "but you never know for sure what she's up to."

Lorraine shook her head and sighed. Her eyes dropped to her lap. Her jaw clenched. Then her expression softened. She looked up at me again. "You know what I like about you?"

Her question surprised me. Before I could even think what to say, she went on. "You stand up for what you believe in. You're kind. But I know what I can expect from you."

My breath caught. People-pleaser that I was, standing up to the pressure over showing on Sabbath had been one of the hardest things I'd ever done.

Lorraine smiled. "I know I can trust you."

Occasionally I talked to the director of the Prison Pet Partnership Program. She and Gail were delighted with how quickly Kelah learned. Well, how quickly she learned *most* things. With Kelah not being a retriever by nature, it took major creativity and patience to get her to understand about going after something and bringing it to the trainer. But one day that seemed to click in her mind and she was retrieving items and acting very proud of herself when she delivered them to Gail.

After only three months, the program director telephoned me. "Kelah's ready to meet Joanne," she said. "She's doing all the things Joanne requested. Would you like to come and see how they work together?"

I arrived at the prison a little before Joanne. When Joanne arrived in her electric scooter, she stopped just inside the doors. A look of wonder crossed her face.

Kelah opens a door for Joanne. As a service dog, when Kelah wears her pack, she's at work.

Later I asked Joanne what she was thinking at that moment. "She's so big!" she said. "And so beautiful!" Then: "Look! She's helping her trainer take off her sweater! And she's loving it."

Joanne and Kelah were introduced. Gail worked with them in the prison and a volunteer went with them to practice out in the community.

I watched a bond between Joanne and Kelah begin to develop. In only three days, Kelah went home with Joanne.

Joanne called every day at first. "She held my wallet today at the grocery store while I got out the money." "She's doing really well at helping me get my sweater off." But it wasn't all smooth sailing. "She won't bring me the phone. She did for Gail. How come she won't for me?"

"Give it some time," I encouraged. "Or maybe give the director a call and see if you can talk to Gail."

A few days later Joanne said, "I'm calling to tell you Kelah just brought me the phone! She's such a good girl! She's so wonderful!"

Again and again, I thanked God for the joy of sharing.

A couple months later I got extra busy. Summer, Kelah's littermate, had a litter of Zion's puppies. Seven puppies.

But I still had time for Joanne. Her phone calls still came at least three times a week. They were full of delight.

Suddenly the calls stopped. A week went by. I called and left a message on her answering machine. "Joanne, please call me." No call. I left a couple more messages. No calls. Two weeks went by with no phone calls from Joanne. This wasn't like her. Since she'd had Kelah, every time they were going to be gone, even for a day, she told me. Something wasn't right.

Something Wasn't Right

BETWEEN PRAYING FOR JOANNE, leaving pleas on her answering machine for her to call me, and wondering whatever had happened to her and Kelah, I cared for seven energetic puppies.

When they were first born, I put different color collars on each and identified them as such—Red Collar, Yellow Collar, etc. With seven black puppies, it was about the only way to keep track of them individually.

The first week I weighed the puppies every day—the average giant schnauzer puppy weighs one pound two ounces. They're about the size of a large potato. Some puppies double their weight in the first week. After that I weighed and measured their height every week.

As the puppies grew, I began training them. For instance, when they wanted to come in from outside, if they jumped on the sliding-glass door, I wouldn't open it. I opened the door for them only when they sat at the door.

Puppy raising was a lot of work, but it was fun to see their personalities develop. From the first, Blue Collar was an unusual little lady. Most puppies, when picked up and held on their backs, squirm and wiggle. Some nervous pups never get over the squirming. Many, however, when repeatedly held securely on their back, gain trust in humans.

From day one, when I picked up Blue Collar and held her on her back, she lay there perfectly calm and looked into my eyes as if to say, "Hi. You're my master, aren't you? I'd like to get to know you better."

All the while I was thinking, *No! I'm not your master! I'm not keeping any puppies! I'm too busy as it is! I don't have time to raise a puppy!*

On the floor Blue Collar was as alert and playful as any of the pups. But when I held her, her eyes focused on me.

One day when I visited a friend who was likely in her final weeks of fighting cancer, we talked about the puppies. She begged me to bring them with me next time I came.

The pups were 8 weeks old when I took them to visit Grace. Each was about the size of a full-grown miniature schnauzer. I toted the big box inside and set it by Grace's hospital bed in her living room. She rolled over and peered down into the box. The puppies bounced around, pulled each other's ears, and wrestled awkwardly.

Grace smiled at the puppies' antics. "Thank you for bringing them, Joy," she said. "It's so fun to see life."

We visited and watched. Finally she needed to roll back onto her back. "May I touch one?" she asked.

"Sure." I leaned over the box. *Which one would . . . ?* Before I finished the question, I knew that Blue Collar would be best to hold up for Grace to touch. I lifted Blue Collar and set her gently beside my ill friend. I held onto Blue Collar—she was a playful 8-week-old puppy, after all.

Blue Collar snuggled close to Grace's frail side and looked into her eyes. Grace laid her hand on Blue Collar's head. "She's s-o-o-o soft. Oh, look at her eyes."

Blue Collar didn't move. She just stayed snuggled against Grace, gazing into her eyes. I wouldn't have believed that possible of an 8-week-old puppy.

Isn't this what you're breeding for? I heard God whisper.

Yes, I shot back. *But I'm too busy to keep a puppy.*

Grace unknowingly rescued me. "She's so relaxed," she said. "So trusting."

So trusting, God echoed.

As Grace and I talked, her tight voice softened. The lines in her faced visibly relaxed.

"Grace," I said after a bit, "I'd better let you rest now." I reached for Blue Collar.

"Thank you for bringing the puppies," Grace whispered. "You can bring this little gal whenever you come."

A couple days later I finally got word about Joanne. Her son called me at home. "I just got your messages on Mom's answering machine. She fell and broke her ankle. She's been in the hospital. Just got transferred to a rehabilitation hospital in Boise. She'd love to hear from you!" He gave me the contact information.

"Where's Kelah?" I asked.

"She's with Mom," he assured me. "I'd like to tell you more, but Mom will want to. You'll be sure to call her, won't you?"

"Yes!" I assured him. I dialed the number as soon as we hung up.

"Joy! I'm so glad you called!"

"How are you, Joanne? What happened?"

"Well, I'm going to be fine. But if it weren't for your gift, I wouldn't be!"

"Huh?"

"I slipped when I was transferring from my scooter to my bed at home, and fell. My ankle was stuck underneath my scooter. I couldn't get it out, and it hurt so bad. Kelah came right over to me and waited, as if she sensed something was wrong. 'Kelah,' I said. 'Get the phone.' And she marched right to the phone, picked it up, and brought it right to me. I might be dead, still lying right there, if it weren't for Kelah. How can I ever thank you enough, Joy?"

"Joanne," I said swallowing hard. "You just did. I'm so thankful God made it clear to me that she belonged with you. So, where's Kelah now?"

"She's right here beside me. When the ambulance crew were going to take me, I said, 'My dog goes too. She's a service dog. She goes with me everywhere.' So she rode with me in the ambulance.

"She stayed beside me in the hospital," Joanne continued. "In fact, every doctor or nurse had to get past Kelah before they could get to me. When they checked my blood pressure or whatever they did, she'd be right there watching, being sure I was OK with it. And, here, her bed is right beside mine."

"They let her be with you in the hospital?"

"Yes. In fact, she's quite a celebrity. A TV station got wind of a dog in the hospital, and Kelah and I were on TV, then in the newspaper. So the whole area knows Kelah saved my life."

Over the next few days, I thanked God over and over for giving me Kelah. For making her perfect for Joanne. For helping me want to give Kelah to Joanne. For helping Kelah learn what Joanne needed. For helping her retrieve the phone in the emergency!

"'Seek ye first the kingdom of God . . .'" I sang over and over, "'and all these things shall be added unto you.'"

"Thank You, God, for Joanne's safety," I often said. "Sure, the money would have been nice, but my friend's safety is so much more important!"

It was good to talk to Joanne again every few days.

And good to visit Grace every week. Each time, Blue Collar snuggled beside her. Not only did Grace enjoy Blue Collar, but it seemed like when Grace could feel and look at the puppy, she reached deeper into her soul during our conversations.

"Are you resting in Jesus, Grace?" I asked in one of our last visits.

"Yes," she said. She smiled weakly. "That's the only way peace is possible."

That spring as I prepared for teen camp meeting, I pleaded that God would help me forget my nervousness and that He would bless the teens through Zion and me. New illustration ideas came. I started getting excited about sharing with teens.

It turned out Zion was a real hit. And I discovered teens were one of my favorite audiences.

One evening after the meeting one of the girls said, "You must have spent lots and lots of hours training Zion."

I thought back. What I realized surprised me. "No," I said. "Not really. But we've spent lots of time building a good, loving relationship—playing together, going places together, just being together. The more Zion and I know each other, the more he loves to do things for me. So the actual training was really pretty fun and easy."

"Interesting," she responded. Then her eyes brightened. "You know," she said thoughtfully, "that's like with us and Jesus, huh?"

"Yes," I replied. "You're right." We stood in silence, the thought working its way deep into my mind. Finally, I spoke again. "Thank you. You just helped God teach me a really important lesson."

It was just like God the next morning to show me John 17:3: "Now this is eternal life: that they may know you, the only true God, and Jesus Christ, whom you have sent" (NKJV). *Joyful living,* I realized anew, *comes simply from knowing God!*

One night that week the other speaker talked about life's rough times. "If you forget everything I've said all week," he told us, don't forget this one thing. Whatever's going on, just keep coming to Jesus. If you're mad at Him, come to Him and tell Him so. If you feel like yelling at Him, come to Him and yell at Him. If you fail Him, come. Whatever happens, just keep coming to Jesus."

Like Zion, I thought. *He never outgrows coming.*

At home, every time I looked at the puppies a thought needled me. *You ought to keep Blue Collar.*

I tried to ignore the idea. I was busy. Besides taking care of seven puppies and grooming and training other dogs, I'd started training their dad, Zion, to "wave" and "sit up like a bear." His audiences would love it.

"Joy!" Joanne enthused one morning when I called her. "I wish you'd seen what happened! It was just l-l-like a m-m-miracle!"

"What happened?"

"There was a 4-year-old boy here that had done nothing but stare into space since he was in a car accident a month ago. He had head injuries. He could walk, but that was all. He didn't seem to recognize anyone or anything. He wouldn't feed himself. Didn't respond to anything. Had only a vacant stare."

"Yes?"

"A nurse got an idea. Three days ago she took Kelah to see him. Kelah walked right over and put her chin on his shoulder. He blinked when her cold nose touched his ear. After a couple minutes he smiled at Kelah, then threw his arms around her neck. Then he started talking to her.

"Joy," she continued, "you can't believe Kelah. She just seems to know what someone needs. That little boy started talking a blue streak. Put on his own pajamas that night. Dressed himself the next morning. He ate by himself. You should'a seen his mom and dad! This morning they took him home!"

Satisfaction welled up in my heart till it felt like it would burst.

One morning I sensed God saying, *Joy, you really ought to keep Blue Collar. She has a perfect temperament to work with people.*

"B-b-but I don't even have a name for her."

Lovely, I heard. *Altogether Lovely.*

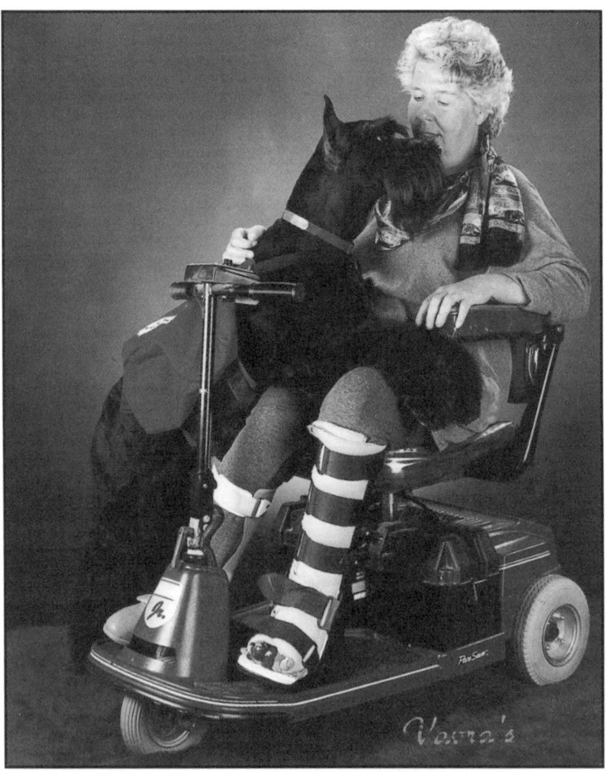

Vavra Photography

Joanne and Kelah adore each other

"Altogether Lovely?" I questioned. "But that's a name for Jesus."

Zion's a heavenly name too. They're doing My work.

"Altogether Lovely," I repeated. "I could call her Lovely."

Before I was through writing in my prayer journal that morning, Blue Collar became Lovely.

Joanne takes Kelah for a walk.

That left six pups to find homes for. I didn't advertise at all. These were Zion's pups. By the time they were 9 weeks old, all but my Lovely pup were sold and I had a waiting list for the next litter.

One day when I called Joanne she was bubbling over again. "Joy, I wish you could see what's happening here. Since that little boy started talking, the nurses have been taking Kelah on evening rounds. The patients love her. There are two teen girls here who were in separate car accidents and are in comas. One nurse started laying Kelah beside each girl for a while each night. Susan's eyes flicker now when they put Kelah in bed with her."

Each conversation with Joanne contained progress reports. "Susan started petting Kelah last night." A couple days later. "Susan opened her eyes and looked at Kelah! And last night the nurse was sure that Jennifer knew it when she put Kelah beside her." Then, "Susan woke up and started talking to Kelah!"

The next week I was headed to Boise to show Zion. "I'll be in to visit you Friday as soon as I can get away from the show," I said. "Do you think they'd let me see Kelah at work while I'm down there?"

You'll Never Believe

AS SOON AS I COULD GET AWAY from the dog show, I headed to the rehabilitation hospital.

"Joy, this is the perfect day for you to come!" Joanne enthused.

"Why?"

"Sit down," Joanne said. She motioned toward a chair. "Just wait a minute." She rang the nurse's call buzzer. "Joy's here," she said.

"What's going on?" I asked.

"Patience, patience." Joanne hushed me with a gleam in her eye.

Soon three women entered the room. A nurse led the way. A teen girl followed, limping slightly. The third woman looked like an older version of the teenager.

"Joy," Joanne said, "it's my absolute pleasure to introduce you to Susan."

"Susan!" I gasped.

A million unasked questions hung in the air. Then we were all talking at once.

The soft feel of Kelah next to her was the first thing Susan remembered after seeing the other car heading directly toward hers. Then seeing Kelah's loving eyes looking into her own. After being in a coma for three weeks, over the next few days

Susan talked, sat up, fed herself, walked, dressed, read, did math. She was fine. That day she was leaving for home with her mother. Since I was coming, they waited.

It was a tearful goodbye. Tears of joy!

I still didn't have the $5,000.00 Kelah could have sold for. But with God's help, we were making it. If Kelah had been worth a million dollars and I could have seen the future, I still would have given her to Joanne—in a minute!

On the way home, I couldn't stop thanking God.

Vavra Photography

Joanne and I admire Kelah. If Kelah had been worth $1 million and I could have seen the future, I still would have given her to Joanne . . . in a minute.

Jennifer's recovery was slower. But eventually she, too, opened her eyes and looked at Kelah, then began petting her and talking to her. Unfortunately, Jennifer's spinal cord had been injured. Though she was awake, barring a miracle she'd be in a wheelchair the rest of her life. But the fact that she could go home in a wheelchair, was a miracle in itself. A miracle aided by Kelah.

After Joanne and Kelah had been home a couple months,

Joanne said, "Joy, now Kelah gets things I need without my even telling her to. If something falls, she picks it up. The other day a pen rolled under the refrigerator. Kelah went over, lay down, batted it out with her paw, and brought it back to me—without my ever saying a word."

A couple months later Joanne said, "Joy, you'd never guess what Kelah's doing now."

"What?"

"I've gotten spasms in my legs for a while."

"Yeah."

"Somehow, Kelah senses it when I get a spasm. She gets up out of her bed without my ever saying a word. She jumps up beside me, lays down by the leg that has the spasm, and pushes her warm body against it. She stays right there and puts pressure on the area in spasm until it's relieved. Then she gets up and goes back to her own bed."

"How'd you get her to do that?"

"I didn't do a thing. She did it totally on her own," Joanne said. "In fact, I thought it was an accident the first couple times. But it's happened every time I've gotten a spasm for the past three weeks."

The next morning as I played in the yard with Zion, God whispered, *I didn't make Kelah to share her life with three other dogs and all the commotion at your house. I made her perfect to be with Joanne—one on one.*

I remembered the pillows and papers Kelah had chewed, the toys and slippers that disappeared, the numerous times her nose was at my hand when I was trying to get something done. I'd often sighed in desperation and put Kelah outside in the fenced yard.

What Kelah really needed was attention, a one on one relationship to which she could respond. Now she was happy—she'd found her master and her mission.

Zion was doing well with "Wave" and "Sit up like a bear." Just thinking about the children, I could almost hear a collective "oo-oo-ooh."

In the spring, Lovely was old enough to enter puppy shows. At Spring Circuit she got the same kind of attention Zion had.

Zion was getting pretty good at waving and sitting up like a bear. We would put that to use soon, since I'd agreed to take him to a camp meeting in the summer and share with the kindergarten, primary, junior, and teen classes.

One afternoon Zion and I went out into our large fenced yard. We reinforced "Come," "Watch," "Wave," and "Sit up like a bear." We played ball and tug of war. Then I released Zion to play on his own.

He ran across the yard at full speed. To me, just seeing him run was a beauty to behold. He was large and muscular. Watching him run in the grass was almost like watching a small horse race through a pasture.

He stopped and sniffed at some scent. Then ran again. I turned to check out the buds on the lilacs near the fence.

Suddenly I heard a wrenching yelp. I wheeled around. Zion was on the ground.

I raced toward him. With his front paws my majestic giant schnauzer pulled himself toward me, inches at a time. His back legs dragged uselessly behind. Terror filled his eyes. He cried in pain.

The End?

ZION'S PITIFUL CRY SENT CHILLS up my spine. My heart pounded in my throat.

When I got to him and he lay still, his crying softened slightly.

"Zion," I commanded. "Stay!"

Recognition registered in his eyes.

I ran toward the house. My thoughts raced faster than my legs. *How am I going to get him across the field to the car? . . . How will I get him into the car? . . . This is the end . . . the end of the ministry . . . the end of showing.* My feet seemed to move in slow motion. "God, Zion's been Your dog all along. Do what's best. But, please, take his awful pain away."

I phoned the vet. "Zion's paralyzed, I blurted."

"Bring him right in," she said.

I grabbed the keys and ran for the car. Started it, turned it around, and gunned it. I'd been gone from Zion for 10 minutes. "Please don't let him hurt too much," I prayed. "You know I don't want to lose Zion. But whatever happens, I'll still praise You.

As I pulled up to the gate, my heart nearly stopped. I couldn't let go of the steering wheel. I stared in disbelief.

Zion stood at the gate . . . on all fours.

I blinked. He still stood at the gate. Rather than being flat, however, his back humped up in the middle, like the shape of a tent.

"Praise God!" I said. It was the first time I'd ever praised God that one of my dogs disobeyed!

I got out of the car and walked toward Zion slowly. I didn't want to get him excited. As I led him to the car, he walked with a strange, stiff-legged gait. On the road, when the car hit a bump, he cried softly.

Dr. Kruger waited outside when we pulled up. "He was standing up when I got back to the yard!" I said as I walked around the car. We lifted Zion gently onto the ground. He stood briefly with arched back, then walked stiffly to a tree. He lifted one hind leg and marked the tree. Then he walked to the other side, lifted the other hind leg, and marked it again.

"Did you see that?" Dr. Kruger questioned.

"Yeah."

If I'd been the only one to see it, I might have questioned my senses. But we both saw it. Both back legs worked. Zion's spine would even allow him to balance on one hind foot at a time—either one. I'd never been so happy to see a dog potty!

After Dr. Kruger examined and X-rayed Zion, she said, "Looks like nothing's broken. But I'm sure he's bruised his spine. Obviously he's walked. I think he'll continue to be able to. But I can't give you any guarantee what it'll look like when he does."

"I'm just glad he can," I said. "I thought I was bringing him in to have you put him down."

"I heard that in your voice," she said. Her eyes brimmed with moisture. She knew Zion well. Knew about our ministry.

She gave Zion a shot at the injury site to help reduce the swelling so it wouldn't injure the spinal cord any worse. "Keep life really easy for him," she instructed. "Let me see him in the office in a week. Unless, of course, he doesn't respond the way you think he ought to. Call me anytime."

"Thank You, God!" I praised on the way home. "Thank

You for giving him back to me." We reached the edge of our little town and headed out into the country toward home. "But why did You give him back?" I asked. The tires hummed against the pavement. "Will he be able to do the ministry anymore? What about the camp meeting we were supposed to go to? This is April. camp meeting's in June. There's only two months. Shall I cancel?"

Wait, I sensed. *For now, just wait.*

"All right, Lord; I'll wait. You work out whatever is best."

I glanced in the rear view mirror. Zion lay in the back seat. A warm glow welled up in my chest. "Thank You, God, that I'm taking him home alive!"

When Del got home, he stopped only a few steps inside the door. "What's wrong with Zion?"

I recounted the afternoon. "God had to have healed him," I finished.

"Don't get your hopes up too high," Del warned.

"I don't really have any hopes at all," I admitted. "All I know is that he was paralyzed. And now he's not."

Zion walked stiffly across the room, his back arched. He lay down awkwardly on his bed.

"I'm just glad I didn't have to have him put to sleep," I said. "Whatever life he has from now on, whatever he's able to do, it's clearly a gift from God."

By the end of the week Zion's gait had improved. At the end of the second week Dr. Kruger said, "If I hadn't believed in miracles, I'd have to now! He's already walking better than I thought he might ever walk again."

The best we could figure what had happened was that while Zion was running full tilt, he stumbled in a rough spot in the yard. As powerful as he was, it twisted his back.

With Zion doing so well, we resumed practice for camp meeting. Afraid of putting pressure on his back, I put off asking him to wave. And I definitely skipped "Sit up like a bear." That would be hard on his back. He might never be able to do that.

That spring Natalie, a young friend of our family, was fighting leukemia. During treatment she and her family stayed at the Ronald McDonald House near Children's Hospital in Seattle. They got acquainted with other ill children and their families. "You've got to come and bring Zion," her mother urged. "These kids would love him!"

Because of Zion's accident, I postponed going until Natalie's mom called again. "We're almost through with treatment. We get to take Natalie home next week. Can you bring Zion before we leave?"

Six weeks after Zion's accident we headed for Ronald McDonald house. A group of children and parents gathered in the large living room. Zion did tricks for them. I answered all kinds of questions. Yes, Zion was a show dog. Yes, he had won many awards; he'd even been in the top 10 of all the giant schnauzers in the nation for five years in a row. I told them Zion's favorite thing was to visit kids.

The children gathered around Zion and showered him with petting and patting. Bright eyes—the children's and the dog's—showed delight.

Eventually everyone but Jordie left. She, Natalie, their mothers, and Zion and I went outside in the sunshine.

Jordie was a precocious 5-year-old. She'd lost all but a few strands of hair. She rode in a large stroller—multiple tumors up and down both legs made walking impossible. She hadn't been able to stand by herself for several months. Zion sat by the stroller and Jordie gave him a good dose of loving. She wore an almost-constant smile.

We adults got caught up in our conversation. Suddenly Jordie's mom gasped. "Jordie, be careful—"

"It's OK, Mommy," Jordie interrupted. "Zion will help me."

We watched, barely breathing. Jordie had already scooted forward in her stroller. She grabbed Zion's neck and pulled herself up.

God, don't let Zion move, I prayed silently.

Standing on tiptoe and holding tightly to Zion, Jordie turned and looked at us adults with a smile that could have melted an iceberg.

Zion didn't even flinch as Jodie grabbed his neck and pulled herself up. After I caught my breath, I joined them . . . just in case.

When I Thought We Were Done

A WEEK BEFORE CAMP MEETING I could still see a slight arch in Zion's back. But it wasn't noticeable to most people. I decided to see if Zion still remembered how to wave and if he would be able to. "Wave and say goodbye," I said as I waved to help remind him.

Instead, Zion sat up like a bear!

I stood, almost paralyzed myself. He didn't act like it hurt him. he'd learned "Wave" and "Sit up like a bear" about the same time, and we hadn't practiced them for a while. We'd have to get them straightened out. Some practice would take care of that. "Thank You, God!" I whispered.

During the week at camp meeting, Zion and I visited the different children's and teens' classes. Friday afternoon the children's leader hunted me down. "I've got parents saying, 'What's going on in the children's classes?' Their kids are all excited about Zion and talking about him. The parents want to see him too. Sabbath afternoon would you do a review for the kids and parents?"

I gulped. "I-I-I guess so."

"Good," she responded. "We'll get it arranged. Plan on an hour."

An hour? I thought. I was used to telling children's stories. Seven minutes. Maybe 10. Fifteen at the most. I headed for our trailer.

"Lord, I didn't come prepared for this. You're going to have to help me put it together!"

Recently I'd started memorizing Scripture verses. God used them now. Others had been nervous too. Moses, for example. But God told him, "Now go; I will help you speak and will teach you what to say" (Exodus 4:12).

"You've done that for me before. Will You do it for me again?"

"My grace is sufficient for you, for my power is made perfect in weakness" [2 Corinthians 12:9].

"Well, I've got the weakness part down pat. I need Your strength."

"So do not fear, for I am with you; do not be dismayed, for I am your God. I will strengthen you and help you; I will uphold you with my righteous right hand" [Isaiah 41:10].

I pictured Jesus holding me up with His right hand as I stood in front of the children and a few of their parents. "It's a privilege to get to share Jesus," I reminded myself. "Why do I get so nervous sometimes?"

I looked, unseeing, out the trailer window, then spoke slowly as the thought formed. "I get nervous when I forget what I'm doing and start thinking about myself."

It was true. I looked upward. "OK, God. Keep my focus on You." I set to making notes.

Sabbath afternoon I stepped onto the platform with Zion at my side and looked out at the audience. It was *not* just the kids we'd taught all week, plus a few parents. Children filled the first several rows of chapel seats and overflowed, cross-legged, in front of the seats and down the center aisle. Adults filled the rest of the seats and stood in the back of the auditorium.

Knees knocking and hands trembling, I sent a silent SOS heavenward. *Help!*

The words of Philippians 4:13 flashed into my mind. "I can

do all things through Christ which strengtheneth me" (KJV).

God, I'll depend on Your strength!

"Good afternoon," I said. "We've visited you children before. The first thing we talked about was the most important word I can teach Zion. Do you remember that word?"

"Come!" the children chorused.

I reviewed the five words Zion had demonstrated during the week—"come," "look," "wait," "give," and "ready." I included some stories the children hadn't heard.

Zion and I had never presented all five of those words together. But Zion did his part like a pro. He didn't act as if his back bothered him a bit. At the end, as children 4 to 94 flocked around Zion, a few children asked questions. What surprised me was the response from the adults. They hung around and talked with me for a long time. "You made spiritual principles so clear!" one said.

The last man said, "I've never heard the gospel presented so simply. What you gave was really the plan of salvation in five words."

I'd never thought about it like that. But if you "come" to Jesus—over and over in every kind of circumstance, if you "look" to Him—watch Him, not allowing anything to distract you; if you "wait" before Him every day to receive His strength and direction; if you "give" your heart to him and your service to those around you, you will be "ready"; whenever Jesus comes.

When I thought we were finished, God was just getting started. From that point, requests poured in. "Would you talk to our youth?" "Would you bring Zion to our Vacation Bible School?" "Would you and Zion come to our church and do a sermon?"

A sermon?

The idea of a sermon caught me off guard. *But God is able to do in me whatever He asks of me,* I reminded myself.

The title of the sermon was "Training for Heaven in Five Words." Old and young alike watched and listened.

"You make the Christian life so easy to understand," one woman said afterward. A man said, "That's as clear as I've ever understood God wanting to have a friendship with me." An 11-year-old boy said, "That was the best sermon I ever heard. I want Jesus to be my Master."

"Praise the Lord," was all I could say. It wasn't about me. It wasn't about something I was or I'd done. It was about God using an unlikely prospect with an unusual talent.

Three months after Zion's accident, I registered both him and Lovely for a Canadian show. Would he show OK?

Lovely, at 10 months, won the puppy sweepstakes against 50 other giant schnauzer pups. After the show she attracted considerable attention.

Zion still grumbled sometimes. But not only could he still hold his own, he won Best of Breed and took third place in the working group, getting the most points possible in a Canadian competition.

Leaving the ring after Zion's last show in the United States.

One day Lovely showed against a really nice, mature giant. He got the ribbon. When we left the ring, I smiled to the owner. "It was a pleasure to lose to you."

The man nearly lost his teeth.

"He's a nice dog," I explained.

Zion still competed in Canada. As a 7-year-old, he was still winning over dogs half his age.

"Thank you," he stuttered. Then he asked about Lovely.

"She's not just a show dog," I said. "She goes to nursing homes to encourage people, and she goes with me to church and helps me tell stories for children."

Later when I had Zion, a Saint Bernard looked like he might close in on him. I stepped between the dogs. When I looked up, I saw the hard lines on the handler's face. *What if a bigger prize for some dog was all I had to look forward to?* I wondered. I smiled at the handler. She blinked and looked again, like she couldn't fathom warmth.

God, I prayed silently, *reach to her heart. Touch her with Your love somehow.*

Fortunately for me, life had become bigger and better than ribbons and awards.

I'd planned to take Zion to Ronald McDonald House to

see Jordie on our way home. Jordie was scheduled for heart surgery, and I thought Zion might cheer her up. But when we arrived, things had changed. The doctors had done further tests to be sure her little body could stand the trauma of surgery. They found that cancer had hopelessly involved her internal organs. Heart surgery was canceled.

Jordie beamed when she saw Zion. "He's yours for the afternoon," I told her. She squealed with glee. Natalie pushed Jordie in her stroller, with Zion walking alongside. When Jordie lay on the grass beside Zion with her arm around his neck, she whispered her thoughts in his ear. She delighterd in Zion's visit.

"Thank you," her mother said. "Thank you for sharing Zion. Jordie has talked about him ever since you were here before. He's made these tough days so much brighter for her."

Jordie delighted in Zion's visit.

My heart ached for Jordie and her family. The next day they flew home to Alaska. Two weeks later Jordie died.

What a privilege it had been to bring some sunshine to Jordie and her family in their dark days.

Two weeks later Zion and I were back in Canada. At the end of that show Zion needed only one more point to gain Canadian championship. I signed him up for both Friday and Sunday shows a couple weeks later, just in case he didn't win any points the first time. Injury not withstanding, on Friday he got the maximum points possible again—five. He took Best of Breed, then went into the working group and took first place.

What a way to go out! Now Zion had earned American, National, International, and Canadian championships. And *every* win had been an honest win!

At Ronald McDonald house, Zion had time for Jodie's sister, Tory, too. Her family appreciated Zion so much that a couple years later when a baby brother was born, they named him Zion Joseph.

Sunday I went just to observe the show. "Why aren't you showing your dog?" one handler asked.

"Because he's retired," I replied.

"Retired?" he asked incredulously.

"Yes. He is 7 years old, after all."

"Seven?" he asked. "No. He can't be 7."

"Yes, he's 7."

"He doesn't look 7. He looks like he's in his prime. Three. Maybe 4."

He was amazed. And rightly so. The Giants as big as Zion who didn't have good breeding, were often dead by 4. Sometimes even 3.

Another handler saw me without Zion. "Where's your dog?"

"Back in our trailer," I replied.

"Aren't you showing him today?"

"No."

He laughed. "Melinda's going to be cranked when she hears that. She wanted in the worst way to finish her dog's championship, but when she realized Zion was signed up, she knew it wouldn't do her any good to bring her dog. She didn't even come."

Zion still put fear in his competitors.

When I got back to the trailer, I told my gentle giant, "Zion, you retired a true champion. You never have to go in the showring again! You don't have to put up with the other big dogs. And I don't have to worry about your grumbling. Now you can do what you really enjoy doing: going with me when I visit people and tell stories."

I don't know if he got my drift or just liked hearing my voice, but his tail wagged at quite a clip.

Serving and showing. They were totally different. For a while showing and winning had seemed like everything. But the silver bowls and trophies tarnished. They lost their beauty. However, the glow I felt inside from seeing others' delight when I shared Zion grew greater and greater.

CHAPTER 22

Problem Pups

I'D LEARNED SO MUCH THROUGH ZION'S show career and ministry. I thought I'd learned to trust God no matter what. Then there was *the* litter of pups.

I checked out the list of people who had asked for a pup sired by Zion. Fifteen families got excited about the possibility. "Yes, I want a puppy. Just let me know when they're born."

Finally Summer, Kelah's littermate, went into labor. Six healthy puppies were born. But X-rays had shown another, and the mother was still struggling. Finally we made a veterinary run, and one more puppy made its delayed debut.

The last pup was a skinny little runt. I had to take the other puppies away from their mother for a while every few hours so Red Collar could nurse. With the extra care, she thrived.

As soon as I knew we had healthy puppies, I began calling the prospective owners with the glad news. Since we'd not have enough puppies for everyone who wanted one, I started at the top of the list—first come, first served.

"I'm so sorry," caller number one said. "The owners of the big house we were renting sold it unexpectedly, and we just had to move into a tiny apartment. We've been so much looking forward to getting a puppy, but the timing just won't work for us right now."

"No problem," I said. "We have more people who want puppies than we have puppies."

Call number two: "Oh, yes. We want a pup. But it's not going to work right now. My husband was just diagnosed with cancer, and we'll be spending a lot of time on the road getting treatment for him. It wouldn't be fair to the pup to take one right now."

Call number three: "I have to go out of town next week for heart surgery. When I talked to the doctor about all the possibilities, I asked about getting a puppy. He said, 'No way. Don't even think about a puppy for at least six months.'"

One by one all 15 prospective puppy owners gave me their apologies and their legitimate reasons why they couldn't take a puppy just then.

Day by day I made sure little Red Collar got a chance to nurse. Before long she was catching up to the others in size. And Red Collar had more energy than the rest of the crew put together. She was a pesky little critter—very loving, always wanting attention, always on the move. She got into everything. She was like a hyperactive child.

"Who'll ever want Red Collar?" I worried. "At the rate she's growing, I may be stuck with a hyperactive house horse for the rest of my life!"

Altogether Lovely

I got away to a couple nearby shows. Lovely gained points toward her championship. She attracted attention much like her father, Zion, had. She too had a royal bearing.

After one show a giant schnauzer owner looked at Lovely and asked, "Is she Zion's pup?"

"Yes."

"What's her name?"

"Lovely," I said. "Altogether Lovely."

She knelt down and felt her build. "That's a perfect name for her!" she said. "She's built perfect. I saw the way she moves. She really is altogether lovely."

A treat in the hand captures Lovely's attention as we wait to enter the ring.

As far as training was concerned, I'd learned a lot at Zion's expense. One day I bemoaned my mistakes to another dog trainer. "Some say every trainer ruins their first dog," she said. "You definitely didn't ruin Zion. But you do know some things you can do better this time around."

For one thing, I exposed Lovely to other dogs after she was 6 months old. But I carefully chose what dogs to introduce her to so it would be a positive experience.

Because I knew clicker training, I started training Lovely with positive reinforcement from the first. She wanted to please me even more than Zion had at that age.

At one show Lorraine shook her head. "Breeders spend a lifetime breeding for one dog as good as Zion. You got two!"

"I feel so blessed!" I told her.

"God must have wanted you to have another grand dog," she said, "so your ministry could continue longer."

Lovely follows in her father's winning footsteps.

Wherever I talked with dog fanciers, I asked if they knew anyone that was in the market for a giant schnauzer puppy. No one did.

I had hoped to have all the puppies to their new owners when the pups were between 8 and 9 weeks old. Instead, I still had every puppy. Seven bouncy pups that needed to be fed, watered, pottied, and trained. I had to admit that when all seven puppies sat in a row outside the sliding-glass door waiting to come in, they were downright cute. But I was tired of being a puppy nursemaid.

"God," I prayed, "how do I get rid of these pups?"

I thought of putting an ad in a Seattle newspaper. But I dismissed the thought. *Zion's puppies shouldn't have to be sold in newspaper ads.*

"A little pride?" I asked myself. I tried to shush the thought.

Over and over I sensed God saying, "Put an ad in a Seattle paper."

When the puppies were 11 weeks old, I put an ad in a Seattle Sunday paper. I didn't get one call about puppies.

At 3 months, we still had seven time-consuming, energy-absorbing, fast-growing, eat-you-out-of-house-and-home puppies.

Frankly, I was getting disgusted. Eight mornings after the ad, while I was out pottying the pups I told God just what I thought. I'd done everything I could think of. "Why don't *You* sell them?" I challenged.

Silence.

After a moment I blundered on: "And what will You ever do with Red Collar?"

The puppies finished their errand and lined up at the door. As the last one entered, the phone rang.

"Hello," I said.

"Hello," a deep, warm male voice responded. "Do you by any chance still have any giant schnauzer puppies?"

My heart nearly stopped. "Y-e-s," I said.

"Do you have a really active puppy?"

I just knew he'd say, "I don't want that one." But I had to answer honestly. "Y-e-s."

"Wonderful!" he shot back. "If you have the right pup, that's the one I want!"

I caught my breath. I answered his questions till he was satisfied we had the puppy for him. As desperate as I was to sell any puppy, *especially* Red Collar, there were a couple essentials. Many dogs got run over because of a particular lack. "Do you have a fenced yard?" I asked.

"Ma'am, is three acres enough?"

"Yes, that's enough."

"I've been hunting a giant schnauzer with a good temperament for months. Had the yard fenced so we'd be ready when we found the right one."

"One more thing," I said. "If a dog won't obey, it can get pretty hard to live with. That's a major reason why people get tired of a dog and abandon it. Especially big dogs.

"Yes?"

"I require that my puppies and their owners take a basic obedience class. Will that be a problem?"

"I've already registered my puppy for a class," he said. "I just need to get the puppy."

"Wonderful!" I said. "Looks like you found your puppy."

"I'm going to Africa for two weeks," the man said. "While I'm gone, could you make the arrangements for flying the puppy to Birmingham, Alabama? As soon as I'm back and know what the total costs will be, I'll send you half the money. Then you can ship our puppy. When I've gotten her, I'll send the rest of the money."

"Birmingham, Alabama?" I asked. "How'd you find out about my puppies?"

"I travel a lot. Was in Seattle a week ago Sunday, picked up a newspaper, and saw your ad on the way home."

We finalized the arrangements.

"I'll call you as soon as I'm back from Africa," he said. "Now, you will be sure to save the really active puppy for me, won't you."

"Yes, sir, I'll save the really active one."

We hung up. I collapsed by my bed and bawled. "God," I said, when I regained a bit of composure, "I believe You."

I grabbed my Bible and opened it to Jeremiah 29:11: " 'For I know the plans I have for you,' declares the Lord, 'plans to prosper you and not to harm you, plans to give you hope and a future.' "

"Your plans are amazing, Lord!" I said. "Always for my good."

I'd pondered that scripture just moments when I heard God whisper, *Ephesians 3:20.*

Still savoring the first text, I grabbed the other Bible on my nightstand. "Now to Him [Christ] who is able to do exceedingly abundantly above all that we ask or think, according to the power that works in us" (NKJV).

"Exceedingly abundantly," I repeated. "Bigger than anything I could ever dream up in my wildest imagination!" I sucked in a deep breath. "But it's not just plans!" I exulted. "You have the power to accomplish them . . . exceedingly abundantly."

"O God," I prayed. "I trust *all* these puppies with you. I worked so hard at trying to sell them my way. When will I learn just to trust You? To rest in You no matter what?"

I trained Red Collar to follow some basic commands—sit, down, stay—and attached a video to her crate that showed the commands. The dog/money transfer went smoothly. The family was delighted with their dog. I praised God.

"I still can't imagine why anyone would want a puppy as active as Red Collar," I told Del. "What if they didn't realize *how* active 'really active' was?"

Del winked. "Well, I guess you'll get a call back." He grinned.

I shivered. "It's not funny!" I moaned.

A dog breeder's worst nightmare is that someone who bought a puppy will decide they don't want it after all.

"God," I prayed that night, "I don't ever want to hear from Red Collar's new owners again."

Days later on the telephone, the rich Alabama accent I'd come to recognize in our puppy dealing said, "Mrs. Matthews, we've got a problem with our puppy."

Perfect

MY HEART SANK. MY BREATH CAUGHT in my throat. Just to think about getting Red Collar back set my mind zipping from worry to worry.

Then I caught myself. *Calm down,* I said to me. *I've decided I'm going to trust God no matter what. This is one of those no-matter-what's. God is big enough to handle anything—even Red Collar.*

I closed my eyes and sucked in a deep breath. "What's the problem?"

"My daughter keeps trying to steal my puppy," he said. "Do you by any chance still have one more for sale?"

On the other end of the phone line, my relief must have sounded like a tire going flat. I didn't tell him I still had six! But he told me what his daughter wanted, and we decided on Yellow Collar.

Feeling brave, I ventured, "So your puppy must be working out OK?"

"Fantastic!" he exclaimed. "I'm the principal of a private school. We have kids from kindergarten through high school. I wanted a dog that would go to school with me every day and interact with the kids. Princess loves everybody, and they all love her. I know it would take a pretty energetic dog to handle the rough and tumble of the most active kids. Princess is absolutely perfect!"

My heart smiled.

It didn't take long to finalize the arrangements. We already knew what it cost to ship a puppy to Birmingham. He wired the money. I shipped the puppy. They were as thrilled with Yellow Collar as they had been with Red Collar.

"God," I prayed, "I don't know a soul who wants a pup. But I'm going to stay out of the way. I'm going to wait on You, no matter what."

Out of the blue a lady who'd met Joanne and Kelah telephoned. She wanted a puppy. She knew someone who wanted another one. One after another, in two weeks, each puppy went to its home—homes all over the country that I had no way of knowing a thing about. And each new owner was ecstatic about their new pup.

One of the neat things about God is that He never runs out of things to teach me through my dogs. Like Red collar. I'd thought she was a mistake. But God doesn't make junk.

In fact, that was really like Kelah, too. The pesky pup just needed to find the right master and mission. And like Zion. God doesn't make junk.

Vavra Photography

What a plan!

H'mmm. God didn't make junk when He made me, either. For a long time I thought I was junk—such a plain Jane. And a talent with animals seemed like such a weird gift. I didn't think God would ever be able to use that. But He made me perfect too. Perfect for a specific job. Perfect for a ministry unlike any other.

If I could have planned my life, I would never in a million years have been able to dream up anything half as exciting or wonderful as God planned!

Epilogue

WHEN ZION TWISTED HIS BACK and was paralyzed, I was sure our ministry was finished. But God is full of surprises. He healed Zion. And that was when our ministry really took off.

Phone calls came more and more frequently. On Sabbath Zion and I might be sharing in a church with 30 members or 1,000. On Tuesday in a school chapel or Vacation Bible School. On the Fourth of July, the two of us riding a float in a parade, with Zion waving his paw to everyone along the route. The next weekend we might be the presenters at a women's retreat. Or a teen retreat.

The first time Zion and I sat under the hot lights of television, it took my breath away for an instant. Three cameras moved in and focused on us. The producer and camera operators busied themselves with final adjustments.

"Don't be nervous, Joy," the host quipped. "It's only international television."

I grinned and looked down at Zion. His bright black eyes rolled up toward me. He was perfectly comfortable and confident—he was beside his master.

My heart pounded in my ears. I wondered if the lump in my throat would swallow my voice. *Relax,* I told myself. *Remember how you got here. It'll be fine—your Master is beside you, too.*

When I was introduced, my voice was strong. God gave me the words to tell people around the globe that God wants to be their best Friend. That He has the perfect plan for every person. That living for Him is by far the best way to go!

As Zion aged, I trained Lovely to demonstrate the same lessons Zion always had, plus some new things.

"Is Zion getting old?" a young boy asked after Lovely demonstrated the first half of a program.

"Yes," I said.

"It seems like Zion is pretty special to you," he added.

"You're right," I agreed. "Zion is pretty special to me.

Zion and I watch Zion Junior getting an early start at loving kids.

There's a reason why. You see, Zion is my salvation. In learning how to be a good master for Zion, I learned that God is a wonderful Master for me. In learning about Zion, I learned to love God. And no matter how old Zion gets, or even if he dies, that's a gift that can never be taken away."

Del and I with Lovely, Tazz, Zion, and four-month-old Zion-Junior.

Lovely began doing more of the programs. Then I got a new puppy, Zion's grandson. When Del and I brought Zion Junior home, he was the exact weight and height that Zion had been at the same age. I marveled as Zion Junior grew. For weeks their sizes were identical. If it was possible for a dog to be as good as Zion and Lovely, Zion Junior was that dog, in both structure and temperament.

Lorraine had been amazed that I could have two dogs the quality of Zion. Now I had three. It had to be a God thing. God must want the ministry to continue. There's simply no other explanation.

Giant trio—Lovely, Zion, and Zion Junior

Epilogue

At age 11½ years, Zion died peacefully in my arms. Though I missed him terribly at first, his gift to me and to thousands around the world still warms my heart.

Lovely continues the ministry. Zion Junior is learning quickly and carrying part of the load. God continues to surprise me, to strengthen me, to give me joy greater than anything I thought possible.

If you'd like Joy Matthews' and God's dogs to visit your church, school, youth group, retreat, camp meeting, parade, or some other event you and God dream up, contact her through her Web site:
www.zionjoysministry.com